A Classification System for Church Libraries

Based on the Dewey Decimal
Classification System®

CONVENTION PRESS
Nashville, Tennessee

ISBN #: 0-8054-9618-1

5120-44

Printed in the United States of America

Church Media Library Program
The Sunday School Board of the Southern Baptist Convention
127 Ninth Avenue North
Nashville, TN 37234

INTRODUCTION

This classification system for church libraries includes the numbers from the Dewey Decimal Classification System which are most often used in church media libraries. The Dewey System is the recognized system for arranging media in a church's library. Originally used to give call numbers to books, the system is now recommended for any format in the collection which needs to be arranged by subject.

Numbers have been selected from the *Abridged Dewey Decimal Classification and Relative Index, edition 12* and *Dewey Decimal Classification 200 Religion Class (unabridged), edition 20.* Some changes which appear in the 21st edition of the unabridged Dewey have also been included. These changes appear in gray shaded areas. Note that not all changes between the 20th and 21st editions of Dewey are reflected in this work.

Notes appear throughout the schedules – especially in the 200s – which reflect the unique application of some numbers in the church library setting. These notes have been adapted from the book *Using the Dewey Decimal Classification System* from *The Church Media Library Series.*

Origin of the Dewey System

The Dewey System was devised by Melvil Dewey in the 1870s. Dewey was a librarian who used the system to organize his own library's collection.

The Dewey System is based on the subject of the media. Therefore, this classification system allows a cataloger to assign numerical call numbers to media which positions each title in a logical arrangement according to its subject. A shelf arrangement by subject makes a library user-friendly. Once a library user finds one title that will meet a need, perhaps other titles will be found nearby. Classification is simply having a place for everything among items which are alike in subject and format.

Although the Dewey System is used in public, school, and church libraries, numbers may not be used in exactly the same way in all three settings. The unique nature of a church's collection assumes that while all books may not be religious they will reflect only the highest standards, reflecting life as God intended it to be lived. For example, a book on Christian parenting would be classified in a church library in 649 along with other parenting titles. However, in a public setting, anything that mentions religion, even if the subject is parenting, marriage, or finances, will be assigned a number from the 200s, such as 248.4.

Arrangement of the System

The Dewey System divides all areas of knowledge into ten main classes or disciplines. This list of ten classes, or the First Summary, is found on page 5. This summary is the broad outline of the system. Note that 000 is Generalities. This is the class for media that is too broad to relate to just one class, such as a set of general encyclopedias. Other broad subjects, such as how to organize and operate a library, are located in this class.

When a library staff member becomes familiar with these ten classes, any call number on the shelf will automatically identify a title's class simply by observing the first number of the call number. For example, since 200 is religion, any call number which begins with the number 2 is immediately known to be a book about religion.

Dewey then took each of the ten classes and divided each one ten times. These one hundred numbers are listed in the Second Summary on page 6. Note that each of these numbers ends in zero and is therefore considered a broad classification number.

But Dewey then took each number in the Second Summary and divided it into ten parts, thus creating one thousand numbers in the Third Summary. See the Third Summary on page 7. Note the number 220 and its ten divisions in the Third Summary. Note the logic of Dewey's arrangement. The divisions for 220 position media on the shelf in the same arrangement as different parts of the Bible.

Note also, that once Dewey arrived at the Third Summary, he had no more zeros. But he was not out of numbers! In fact, at this point, the possible number of classes for the system reaches infinity because Dewey began to divide numbers decimally. Now, instead of ending with a simple three digit number, an additional decimal place allows a cataloger to create a unique classification number. For example, 226 is Gospels and Acts, but 226.2 is Matthew, 226.3 is Mark , 226.4 is Luke and so on.

How to Use the Dewey System

When classifying any type of media, the same basic questions must be asked. What is this title about and why am I adding it to the library's collection? The latter question will help identify where the title should be found. These steps are necessary because identifying the subject of a title is only the first step. The position in a library indicates also how that subject is treated. For example, a collection may contain several books about *reading*. But a book about *reading* may relate to education, recreation, child development, or library science. For that reason, a subject may be listed in the index more than once because it relates to more than one class or discipline.

Numbers in the Schedules which begin on page 18 contain only the numbers that are needed most often in a church media library. For most church libraries these numbers will be adequate until the collection reaches from 12,000-15,000 titles. When the cataloger begins to feel that more numbers are needed, the *Abridged Dewey Decimal Classification and Relative Index* and *200 Religion Class (unabridged)* may then be secured.

Ways to Use this Book

This work may be used as a companion to *Classification and Cataloging Guide* (available on disk or paper from the Church Media Library Program, address on back of title page) to verify what a specific number means. The two helps together can be used by new workers who are learning to use the system. Catalogers may also use this work to verify call numbers before using any copy cataloging source, including review lists and Cataloging in Publication Data.

To use this book for original cataloging, first, determine the subject of the work and how that subject is treated. Then, formulate a search word or phrase that best captures that subject. Search for that word or phrase in the Relative Index which begins on page 84.

Note that sometimes there are multiple listings for a subject since it may relate to more than one discipline. Choose the entry that appears to be the best choice and note the Dewey number. Notice that the index does not list page numbers but Dewey numbers.

Turn in the Schedules to locate the number. Notice how the number relates to the numbers around it. Read any description of that number and look at the top of the page to check the broader treatment. When the cataloger finds the position in the schedules that corresponds to the position that title should occupy in the library, the number can be written down as the title's call number.

Completing the Call Number

In most church libraries many titles will have the same classification number. To create a more specific place on the shelf for each title, a second line is added to complete the call number. There is not a rule for choosing the second line that applies to all media subjects and formats. It should be based on logic and consistency. For example, for most books, shelf arrangement by author within a call number is logical. Therefore, a call number would be completed with the first three letters of the author's last name.

But is that logical for biographies? Since a reader will be more interested in who the book is about than who wrote it, the call number for a single biography should be completed by the first three letters of the last name of the person about whom the book is written. But this procedure will not work for collective biographies for obvious reasons. Whose name would you use? Therefore, a call number for collective biography is completed by the first three letters of the last name of the writer, compiler, editor, or any person who is responsible for the entire work.

When a Call Number is not a Number

Dewey supplied a number for *everything*. But to make a church's collection more user-friendly, some classifications use letters rather than numbers. For example 813 is a Dewey number for fiction, but church library users find titles simply by looking for F.

While 920 is Dewey's number for biography, church libraries use 920 only for collective biography. Using a B for single biography again simplifies the arrangement. Story collections on a general topic may simply be classified as SC.

Age-level Grouping

A church library is usually at least three complete collections. All materials for ages 0-7 have a C in front of the call number or letters. All materials for ages 8-11 have a J in front of the number or letters. For example, call numbers that are made up of letters follow this plan:

CE	**JF**	**F**
CB	**JB**	**B**
CSC	**JSC**	**SC**

Note that the letters are used consistently from one age group to another except for CE. CE is used for a child's easy-to-read book that does not have a specific subject. Even when the work is a picture book with few words, if a subject just as animals, insects, or seasons can be identified, the collection will be much more valuable when arranged by C plus a Dewey number rather than simply using CE.

Other Media Formats

Some church libraries now use Dewey numbers to assign call numbers for audiovisuals. The Dewey number is selected in exactly the same way as a number for a book. What is the subject? How is the subject treated? For example, a video entitled *Effective Parenting* would be assigned the Dewey number 649 for parenting preceded by VC for videocassette. To complete the call number, the first three letters of the title of the work may be used. Therefore, the call number for such a videocassette would be:

VC
649
Eff

This publication includes selected numbers from Abridged Edition 12 and Unabridged Editions 20 and 21 of the Dewey Decimal Classification that may be of use to Baptist libraries. Some nonstandard Dewey numbers and practices have been included. The full hierarchy is not given, and just a few standard subdivisions are included. Many captions and notes are abbreviated, and most references have been removed. In some cases, add notes have been modified and new notes introduced.

SUMMARIES
First Summary
The Ten Main Classes

000   **Generalities**

100   **Philosophy & psychology**

200   **Religion**

300   **Social sciences**

400   **Language**

500   **Natural sciences & mathematics**

600   **Technology (Applied sciences)**

700   **The arts**   Fine and decorative arts

800   **Literature & rhetoric**

900   **Geography & history**

Second Summary
The Hundred Divisions

000	**Generalities**	**500**	**Natural sciences & mathematics**
010	Bibliography	510	Mathematics
020	Library & information sciences	520	Astronomy & allied sciences
030	General encyclopedic works	530	Physics
040		540	Chemistry & allied sciences
050	General serials & their indexes	550	Earth sciences
060	General organizations & museology	560	Paleontology Paleozoology
070	News media, journalism, publishing	570	Life sciences
080	General collections	580	Plants
090	Manuscripts & rare books	590	Animals
100	**Philosophy & psychology**	**600**	**Technology (Applied sciences)**
110	Metaphysics	610	Medical sciences Medicine
120	Epistemology, causation, humankind	620	Engineering & allied operations
130	Paranormal phenomena	630	Agriculture
140	Specific philosophical schools	640	Home economics & family living
150	Psychology	650	Management & auxiliary services
160	Logic	660	Chemical engineering
170	Ethics (Moral philosophy)	670	Manufacturing
180	Ancient, medieval, Oriental philosophy	680	Manufacture for specific uses
190	Modern Western philosophy	690	Buildings
200	**Religion**	**700**	**The arts Fine and decorative arts**
210	Philosophy & theory of religion	710	Civic & landscape art
220	Bible	720	Architecture
230	Christianity Christian theology	730	Plastic arts Sculpture
240	Christian moral & devotional theology	740	Drawing & decorative arts
250	Christian orders & local church	750	Painting & paintings
260	Christian social theology	760	Graphic arts Printmaking & prints
270	Christian church history	770	Photography & photographs
280	Christian denominations & sects	780	Music
290	Other & comparative religions	790	Recreational & performing arts
300	**Social sciences**	**800**	**Literature & rhetoric**
310	General statistics	810	American literature in English
320	Political science	820	English & Old English literatures
330	Economics	830	Literatures of Germanic languages
340	Law	840	Literatures of Romance languages
350	Public administration	850	Italian, Romanian, Rhaeto-Romanic
360	Social problems & services; association	860	Spanish & Portuguese literatures
370	Education	870	Italic literatures Latin
380	Commerce, communications, transport	880	Hellenic literatures Classical Greek
390	Customs, etiquette, folklore	890	Literatures of other languages
400	**Language**	**900**	**Geography & history**
410	Linguistics	910	Geography & travel
420	English & Old English	920	Biography, genealogy, insignia
430	Germanic languages German	930	History of ancient world
440	Romance languages French	940	General history of Europe
450	Italian, Romanian, Rhaeto-Romanic	950	General history of Asia Far East
460	Spanish & Portuguese languages	960	General history of Africa
470	Italic languages Latin	970	General history of North America
480	Hellenic languages Classical Greek	980	General history of South America
490	Other languages	990	General history of other areas

Third Summary
The Thousand Sections
Generalities

Philosophy and Psychology

100	**Philosophy & psychology**	**150**	**Psychology**
101	Theory of philosophy	151	
102	Miscellany	152	Perception, movement, emotions, drives
103	Dictionaries & encyclopedias	153	Mental processes & intelligence
104		154	Subconscious & altered states
105	Serial publications	155	Differential & developmental psychology
106	Organizations & management	156	Comparative psychology
107	Education, research, related topics	157	
108	Kinds of persons treatment	158	Applied psychology
109	Historical & collected persons treatment	159	

110	**Metaphysics**	**160**	**Logic**
111	Ontology	161	Induction
112		162	Deduction
113	Cosmology (Philosophy of nature)	163	
114	Space	164	
115	Time	165	Fallacies & sources of error
116	Change	166	Syllogisms
117	Structure	167	Hypotheses
118	Force & energy	168	Argument & persuasion
119	Number & quantity	169	Analogy

120	**Epistemology, causation, humankind**	**170**	**Ethics (Moral philosophy)**
121	Epistemology (Theory of knowledge)	171	Ethical systems
122	Causation	172	Political ethics
123	Determinism & indeterminism	173	Ethics of family relationships
124	Teleology	174	Occupational ethics
125		175	Ethics of recreation & leisure
126	The self	176	Ethics of sex & reproduction
127	The unconscious & the subconscious	177	Ethics of social relations
128	Humankind	178	Ethics of consumption
129	Origin & destiny of individual souls	179	Other ethical norms

130	**Paranormal phenomena**	**180**	**Ancient, medieval, Oriental philosophy**
131	Parapsychological & occult methods	181	Oriental philosophy
132		182	Pre-Socratic Greek philosophies
133	Parapsychology & occultism	183	Sophistic & Socratic philosophies
134		184	Platonic philosophy
135	Dreams & mysteries	185	Aristotelian philosophy
136		186	Skeptic and Neoplatonic philosophies
137	Divinatory graphology	187	Epicurean philosophy
138	Physiognomy	188	Stoic philosophy
139	Phrenology	189	Medieval Western philosophy

140	**Specific philosophical schools**	**190**	**Modern Western philosophy**
141	Idealism & related systems	191	Philosophy United States & Canada
142	Critical philosophy	192	Philosophy British Isles
143	Bergsonism & intuitionism	193	Philosophy Germany & Austria
144	Humanism & related systems	194	Philosophy France
145	Sensationalism	195	Philosophy Italy
146	Naturalism & related systems	196	Philosophy Spain & Portugal
147	Pantheism & related systems	197	Philosophy Soviet Union
148	Eclecticism, Liberalism, traditionalism	198	Philosophy Scandinavia
149	Other philosophical systems	199	Philosophy Other geographical areas

Religion

200	**Religion**	**250**	**Christian orders & local church**
201		251	Preaching (Homiletics)
202		252	Texts of sermons
203		253	Pastoral office (Pastoral theology)
204		254	Parish administration
205	[Numbers 201 – 208 relocated to 230s]	255	Religious congregations & orders
206		256	
207		257	
208		258	
209	[Relocated to 270]	259	Pastoral care of families & persons

210	**Philosophy & theory of religion**	**260**	**Social & ecclesiatical theology**
211	Concepts of God	261	Social theology
212	Existence, knowability, attributes of God	262	Ecclesiology
213	Creation	263	Days, times, places of observances
214	Theodicy	264	Public worship
215	Science & religion	265	Sacraments, other rites & acts
216	[deleted]	266	Missions
217		267	Associations for religious work
218	Humankind	268	Religious education
219		269	Spiritual renewal

220	**Bible**	**270**	**History of Christianity & Christian church**
221	Old Testament		
222	Historical books of Old Testament	271	Religious orders in church history
223	Poetic books of Old Testament	272	Persecutions in church history
224	Prophetic books of Old Testament	273	Doctrinal controversies & heresies
225	New Testament	274	History of Christianity in Europe
226	Gospels & Acts	275	History of Christianity in Asia
227	Epistles	276	History of Christianity in Africa
228	Revelation (Apocalypse)	277	History of Christianity in North America
229	Apocrypha & pseudepigrapha	278	History of Christianity in South America
		279	History of Christianity in other areas

230	**Christianity Christian theology**	**280**	**Christian denominations & sects**
231	God	281	Early church & Eastern churches
232	Jesus Christ & his family	282	Roman Catholic Church
233	Humankind	283	Anglican churches
234	Salvation (Soteriology) & grace	284	Protestants of Continental origin
235	Spiritual beings	285	Presbyterian, Reformed, Congregational
236	Eschatology	286	Baptist, Disciples of Christ, Adventist
237		287	Methodist & related churches
238	Creeds & catechisms	288	
239	Apologetics & polemics	289	Other denominations & sects

240	**Christian moral & devotional theology**	**290**	**Comparative religions & other religions**
241	Moral theology		
242	Devotional literature	291	Comparative religion
243	Evangelistic writings for individuals	292	Classical (Greek & Roman) religion
244		293	Germanic religion
245	[deleted]	294	Religions of Indic origin
246	Use of art in Christianity	295	Zoroastrianism (Mazdaism, Pareeism)
247	Church furnishings & articles	296	Judaism
248	Christian experience, practice, life	297	Islam, Babism, Bahai Faith
249	Christian observances in family life	298	
		299	Other religions

Social Sciences

300	**Social sciences**		**350**	**Public administration & military science**
301	Sociology & anthropology			
302	Social interaction		351	Of central government
303	Social processes		352	Of local governments
304	Factors affecting social behavior		353	Of U.S. federal & state governments
305	Social groups		354	Of specific central governments
306	Culture & institutions		355	Military science
307	Communities		356	Foot forces & warfare
308			357	Mounted forces & warfare
309			358	Other specialized forces & services
			359	Sea (Naval) forces & warfare
310	**Collections of general statistics**			
311			**360**	**Social problems & services; association**
312			361	General social problems & welfare
313			362	Social welfare problems & services
314	General statistics of Europe		363	Other social problems & services
315	General statistics of Asia		364	Criminology
316	General statistics of Africa		365	Penal & related institutions
317	General statistics of North America		366	Association
318	General statistics of South America		367	General clubs
319	General statistics of other areas		368	Insurance
			369	Miscellaneous kinds of associations
320	**Political science**			
321	Systems of governments & states		**370**	**Education**
322	Relation of state to organized groups		371	School management; special education
323	Civil & political rights		372	Elementary education
324	The political process		373	Secondary education
325	International migration & colonization		374	Adult education
326	Slavery & emancipation		375	Curriculums
327	International relations		376	[deleted]
328	The legislative process		377	[deleted]
329			378	Higher education
			379	Government regulation, control, support
330	**Economics**			
331	Labor economics		**380**	**Commerce, communications, transportation**
332	Financial economics			
333	Economics of land & energy		381	Internal commerce (Domestic trade)
334	Cooperatives		382	International commerce (Foreign trade)
335	Socialism & related systems		383	Postal communication
336	Public finance		384	Communications Telecommunication
337	International economics		385	Railroad transportation
338	Production		386	Inland waterway & ferry transportation
339	Macroeconomics & related topics		387	Water, air, space transportation
			388	Transportation Ground transportation
340	**Law**		389	Metrology & standardization
341	International law			
342	Constitutional & administrative law		**390**	**Customs, etiquette, folklore**
343	Military, tax, trade, industrial law		391	Costume & personal appearance
344	Labor, social, education, cultural law		392	Customs of life cycle & domestic life
345	Criminal law		393	Death customs
346	Private law		394	General customs
347	Civil procedure & courts		395	Etiquette (Manners)
348	Laws (Statutes), regulations, cases		396	
349	Law of specific jurisdictions & areas		397	
			398	Folklore
			399	Customs of war & diplomacy

Language

400	**Language**		**450**	**Italian, Romanian, Rhaeto-Romanic**
401	Philosophy & theory		451	Italian writing system & phonology
402	Miscellany		452	Italian etymology
403	Dictionaries & encyclopedias		453	Italian dictionaries
404	Special topics		454	
405	Serial publications		455	Italian grammar
406	Organizations & management		456	
407	Education, research, related topics		457	Italian language variations
408	Kinds of persons treatment		458	Standard Italian usage
409	Geographical & persons treatment		459	Romanian & Rhaeto-Romanic
410	**Linguistics**		**460**	**Spanish & Portuguese languages**
411	Writing systems		461	Spanish writing system & phonology
412	Etymology		462	Spanish etymology
413	Dictionaries		463	Spanish dictionaries
414	Phonology & phonetics		464	
415	Grammar		465	Spanish grammar
416			466	
417	Dialectology & historical linguistics		467	Spanish language variations
418	Standard usage Applied linguistics		468	Standard Spanish usage
419	Verbal language not spoken or written		469	Portuguese
420	**English & Old English**		**470**	**Italic languages Latin**
421	English writing system & phonology		471	Classical Latin writing & phonology
422	English etymology		472	Classical Latin etymology
423	English dictionaries		473	Classical Latin dictionaries
424			474	
425	English grammar		475	Classical Latin grammar
426			476	
427	English language variations		477	Old, Postclassical, Vulgar Latin
428	Standard English usage		478	Classical Latin usage
429	Old English (Anglo-Saxon)		479	Other Italic languages
430	**Germanic languages German**		**480**	**Hellenic languages Classical Greek**
431	German writing system & phonology		481	Classical Greek writing & phonology
432	German etymology		482	Classical Greek etymology
433	German dictionaries		483	Classical Greek dictionaries
434			484	
435	German grammar		485	Classical Greek grammar
436			486	
437	German language variations		487	Preclassical & postclassical Greek
438	Standard German usage		488	Classical Greek usage
439	Other Germanic languages		489	Other Hellenic languages
440	**Romance languages French**		**490**	**Other languages**
441	French writing system & phonology		491	East Indo-European & Celtic languages
442	French etymology		492	Afro-Asiatic languages Semitic
443	French dictionaries		493	Non-Semitic Afro-Asiatic languages
444			494	Altaic, Uralic, Hyperborean, Dravidian
445	French grammar		495	Languages of East & Southeast Asia
446			496	African languages
447	French language variations		497	North American native languages
448	Standard French usage		498	South American native languages
449	Provençal & Catalan		499	Austronesian & other languages

Natural Sciences and Mathematics

500	**Natural sciences & mathematics**	550	**Earth sciences**
501	Philosophy & theory	551	Geology, hydrology, meteorology
502	Miscellany	552	Petrology
503	Dictionaries & encyclopedias	553	Economic geology
504		554	Earth sciences of Europe
505	Serial publications	555	Earth sciences of Asia
506	Organizations & management	556	Earth sciences of Africa
507	Education, research, related topics	557	Earth sciences of North America
508	Natural history	558	Earth sciences of South America
509	Historical, geographic, persons treatment	559	Earth sciences of other areas

510	**Mathematics**	560	**Paleontology Paleozoology**
511	General principles of mathematics	561	Paleobotany; fossil microorganism
512	Algebra & number theory	562	Fossil invertebrates
513	Arithmetic	563	Other fossil invertebrates
514	Topology	564	Fossil Mollusca & Molluscoidea
515	Analysis	565	Fossil Arthropoda
516	Geometry	566	Fossil Chordata
517		567	Fossil cold-blooded vertebrates
518		568	Fossil Aves (birds)
519	Probabilities & applied mathematics	569	Fossil mammals

520	**Astronomy & allied sciences**	570	**Life sciences**
521	Celestial mechanics	571	
522	Techniques, equipment, materials	572	Human races
523	Specific celestial bodies & phenomena	573	Physical anthropology
524		574	Biology
525	Earth (astronomical geography)	575	Evolution & genetics
526	Mathematical geography	576	Microbiology
527	Celestial navigation	577	General nature of life
528	Ephemerides	578	Microscopy in biology
529	Chronology	579	Collection and preservation

530	**Physics**	580	**Plants**
531	Classical mechanics Solid mechanics	581	Botany
532	Fluid mechanics Liquid mechanics	582	Seed-bearing plants
533	Pneumatics (Gas mechanics)	583	Dicotyledons
534	Sound & related vibrations	584	Monocotyledons
535	Light & paraphonic phenomena	585	Gymnosperms (Naked-seed plants)
536	Heat	586	Seedless plants
537	Electricity & electronics	587	Pteridophyta (Vascular seedless plants)
538	Magnetism	588	Bryophytes
539	Modern physics	589	Thallophytes & prokaryotes

540	**Chemistry & allied sciences**	590	**Animals**
541	Physical & theoretical chemistry	591	Zoology
542	Techniques, equipment, materials	592	Invertebrates
543	Analytical chemistry	593	Protozoa, Echinodermata, related phyla
544	Qualitative analysis	594	Mollusks & related phyla
545	Quantitative analysis	595	Other invertebrates
546	Inorganic chemistry	596	Vertebrates
547	Organic chemistry	597	Cold-blooded vertebrates
548	Crystallography	598	Birds
549	Mineralogy	599	Mammals

Technology (applied sciences)

600	**Technology (Applied sciences)**	**650**	**Management & auxiliary services**
601	Philosophy & theory	651	Office services
602	Miscellany	652	Processes of written communication
603	Dictionaries & encyclopedias	653	Shorthand
604	Special topics	654	
605	Serial publications	655	
606	Organizations	656	
607	Education, research, related topics	657	Accounting
608	Invention & patents	658	General management
609	Historical, areas, persons treatment	659	Advertising & public relations
610	**Medical sciences Medicine**	**660**	**Chemical engineering**
611	Human anatomy, cytology, histology	661	Industrial chemicals technology
612	Human physiology	662	Explosives, fuels technology
613	Promotion of health	663	Beverage technology
614	Incidence & prevention of disease	664	Food technology
615	Pharmacology & therapeutics	665	Industrial oils, fats, waxes, gases
616	Diseases	666	Ceramic & allied technologies
617	Surgery & related medical specialties	667	Cleaning, color, related technologies
618	Gynecology & other medical specialties	668	Technology of other organic products
619	Experimental medicine	669	Metallurgy
620	**Engineering & allied operations**	**670**	**Manufacturing**
621	Applied physics	671	Metalworking & metal products
622	Mining & related operations	672	Iron, steel, other iron alloys
623	Military & nautical engineering	673	Nonferrous metals
624	Civil engineering	674	Lumber processing, wood products, cork
625	Engineering of railroads, roads	675	Leather & fur processing
626		676	Pulp & paper technology
627	Hydraulic engineering	677	Textiles
628	Sanitary & municipal engineering	678	Elastomers & elastomer products
629	Other branches of engineering	679	Other products of specific materials
630	**Agriculture**	**680**	**Manufacture for specific uses**
631	Techniques, equipment, materials	681	Precision instruments & other devices
632	Plant injuries, diseases, pests	682	Small forge work (Blacksmithing)
633	Field & plantation crops	683	Hardware & household appliances
634	Orchards, fruits, forestry	684	Furnishings & home workshops
635	Garden crops (Horticulture)	685	Leather, fur, related products
636	Animal husbandry	686	Printing & related activities
637	Processing dairy & related products	687	Clothing
638	Insect culture	688	Other final products & packaging
639	Hunting, fishing, conservation	689	
640	**Home economics & family living**	**690**	**Buildings**
641	Food & drink	691	Building materials
642	Meals & table service	692	Auxiliary construction practices
643	Housing & household equipment	693	Specific materials & purposes
644	Household utilities	694	Wood construction Carpentry
645	Household furnishings	695	Roof covering
646	Sewing, clothing, personal living	696	Utilities
647	Management of public households	697	Heating, ventilating, air-conditioning
648	Housekeeping	698	Detail finishing
649	Child rearing & home care of sick	699	

The arts   Fine and decorative arts

700	**The arts Fine and decorative arts**		**750**	**Painting & paintings**
701	Philosophy& theory		751	Techniques, equipment, forms
702	Miscellany		752	Color
703	Dictionaries & encyclopediaa		753	Symbolism, allegory, mythology, legend
704	Special topics		754	Genre paintings
705	Serial publications		755	Religion & religious symbolism
706	Organizations & management		756	
707	Education, research, related topics		757	Human figures & their parts
708	Galleries, museums, private collections		758	Other subjects
709	Historical, areas, persons treatment		759	Historical, areas, persons treatment
710	**Civic & landscape art**		**760**	**Graphic arts Printmaking & prints**
711	Area planning (Civic art)		761	Relief processes (Block printing)
712	Landscape architecture		762	
713	Landscape architecture of trafficways		763	Lithographic (Planographic) processes
714	Water features		764	Chromolithography & serigraphy
715	Woody plants		765	Metal engraving
716	Herbaceous plants		766	Mezzotinting & related processes
717	Structures in landscape architecture		767	Etching & drypoint
718	Landscape design of cemeteries		768	
719	Natural landscapes		769	Prints
720	**Architecture**		**770**	**Photography & photographs**
721	Architectural structure		771	Techniques, equipment, materials
722	Architecture to ca. 300		772	Metallic salt processes
723	Architecture from ca. 300 to 1399		773	Pigment processes or printing
724	Architecture from 1400		774	Holography
725	Public structures		775	
726	Buildings for religious purposes		776	
727	Buildings for education & research		777	
728	Residential & related buildings		778	Fields & kinds of photography
729	Design & decoration		779	Photographs
730	**Plastic arts Sculpture**		**780**	**Music**
731	Processes, forms, subjects of sculpture		781	General principles & musical forms
732	Sculpture to ca. 500		782	Vocal music
733	Greek, Etruscan, Roman sculpture		783	Music for single voices The voice
734	Sculpture from ca. 500 to 1399		784	Instruments & instrumental ensembles
735	Sculpture from 1400		785	Ensembles with one instrument per part
736	Carving & carvings		786	Keyboard & other instruments
737	Numismatics & sigillography		787	Stringed instruments
738	Ceramic arts		788	Wind instruments
739	Art metalwork		789	
740	**Drawing & decorative arts**		**790**	**Recreational & performing arts**
741	Drawing & drawings		791	Public performances
742	Perspective		792	Stage presentations
743	Drawing & drawings by subject		793	Indoor games & amusements
744			794	Indoor games of skill
745	Decorative arts		795	Games of chance
746	Textile arts		796	Athletic & outdoor sports & games
747	Interior decoration		797	Aquatic & air sports
748	Glass		798	Equestrian sports & animal racing
749	Furniture & accessories		799	Fishing, hunting, shooting

Literature and rhetoric

800　Literature & rhetoric
801　Philosophy & theory
802　Miscellany
803　Dictionaries & encyclopedias
804
805　Serial publications
806　Organizations
807　Education, research, related topics
808　Rhetoric & collections of literature
809　Literary history & criticism

810　American literature in English
811　Poetry
812　Drama
813　Fiction
814　Essays
815　Speeches
816　Letters
817　Satire & humor
818　Miscellaneous writings
819

820　English & Old English literatures
821　English poetry
822　English drama
823　English fiction
824　English essays
825　English speeches
826　English letters
827　English satire & humor
828　English miscellaneous writings
829　Old English (Anglo-Saxon)

830　Literatures of Germanic languages
831　German poetry
832　German drama
833　German fiction
834　German essays
835　German speeches
836　German letters
837　German satire & humor
838　German miscellaneous writings
839　Other Germanic literatures

840　Literatures of Romance languages
841　French poetry
842　French drama
843　French fiction
844　French essays
845　French speeches
846　French letters
847　French satire & humor
848　French miscellaneous writings
849　Provençal & Catalan

850　Italian, Romanian, Rhaeto-Romanic literatures
851　Italian poetry
852　Italian drama
853　Italian fiction
854　Italian essays
855　Italian speeches
856　Italian letters
857　Italian satire & humor
858　Italian miscellaneous writings
859　Romanian & Rhaeto-Romanic

860　Spanish & Portuguese literatures
861　Spanish poetry
862　Spanish drama
863　Spanish fiction
864　Spanish essays
865　Spanish speeches
866　Spanish letters
867　Spanish satire & humor
868　Spanish miscellaneous writings
869　Portuguese

870　Italic literatures　　Latin
871　Latin poetry
872　Latin dramatic poetry & drama
873　Latin epic poetry & fiction
874　Latin lyric poetry
875　Latin speeches
876　Latin letters
877　Latin satire & humor
878　Latin miscellaneous writings
879　Literatures of other Italic languages

880　Hellenic literatures　　Classical Greek
881　Classical Greek poetry
882　Classical Greek drama
883　Classical Greek epic poetry & fiction
884　Classical Greek lyric poetry
885　Classical Greek speeches
886　Classical Greek letters
887　Classical Greek satire & humor
888　Classical Greek miscellaneous writings
889　Modern Greek

890　Literatures of other languages
891　East Indo-European & Celtic
892　Afro-Asiatic literatures　Semitic
893　Non-Semitic Afro-Asiatic literatures
894　Ural-Altaic, Paleosiberian, Dravidian
895　Literatures of East & Southeast Asia
896　African literatures
897　North American native literatures
898　South American native literatures
899　Other literatures

Geography and history

900	**Geography & history**		**950**	**General history of Asia Far East**
901	Philosophy & theory		951	China & adjacent areas
902	Miscellany		952	Japan
903	Dictionaries & encyclopedias		953	Arabian Peninsula & adjacent areas
904	Collected accounts of events		954	South Asia India
905	Serial publications		955	Iran
906	Organizations & management		956	Middle East (Near East)
907	Education, research, related topics		957	Siberia (Asiatic Russia)
908	With respect to kinds of persons		958	Central Asia
909	World history		959	Southeast Asia
910	**Geography & travel**		**960**	**General history of Africa**
911	Historical geography		961	Tunisia & Libya
912	Graphic representation of earth		962	Egypt & Sudan
913	Ancient world		963	Ethiopia
914	Europe		964	Northwest African coast & offshore islands
915	Asia		965	Algeria
916	Africa		966	West Africa & offshore islands
917	North America		967	Central Africa & offshore islands
918	South America		968	Southern Africa Republic of South Africa
919	Other areas		969	South Indian Ocean islands
920	**Biography, genealogy, insignia**		**970**	**General history of North America**
921			971	Canada
922			972	Middle America Mexico
923			973	United States
924			974	Northeastern United States
925			975	Southeastern United States
926			976	South Central United States
927			977	North Central United States
928			978	Western United States
929	Genealogy, names, insignia		979	Great Basin & Pacific Slope
930	**History of ancient world**		**980**	**General history of South America**
931	China		981	Brazil
932	Egypt		982	Argentina
933	Palestine		983	Chile
934	India		984	Bolivia
935	Mesopotamia & Iranian Plateau		985	Peru
936	Europe north & west of Italy		986	Colombia & Ecuador
937	Italy & adjacent territories		987	Venezuela
938	Greece		988	Guiana
939	Other parts of ancient world		989	Paraguay & Uruguay
940	**General history of Europe**		**990**	**General history of other areas**
941	British Isles		991	
942	England & Wales		992	
943	Central Europe Germany		993	New Zealand
944	France & Monaco		994	Australia
945	Italian Peninsula & adjacent islands		995	Melanesia New Guinea
946	Iberian Peninsula & adjacent islands		996	Other parts of Pacific Polynesia
947	Eastern Europe Russia		997	Atlantic Ocean islands
948	Northern Europe Scandinavia		998	Arctic islands & Antarctica
949	Other parts of Europe		999	Extraterrestrial worlds

SCHEDULES

000

000   Generalities

004   Data processing and computer science

Class here selection and use of computer hardware; computer systems

Including the Internet

.1   General works on specific types of computers

005   Computer programming, programs, data

Class here text processing

.1   Programming

.3   Programs

Computer software

010   Bibliography

History, identification, description of printed, written, audiovisual, machine-readable materials

011   Bibliographies

016   Bibliographies of works on specific subjects

020   Library and information sciences

021   Relationships of libraries, archives

.7   Promotion of libraries, archives

025   Operations of libraries, archives

.1   Administration

Including finance

.2   Collection development

Including selection policies and procedures; acquisition through purchase, exchange, gift; weeding

.3   Bibliographic analysis and control

Including the catalog and its maintenance

.4   Subject analysis and control

Including subject cataloging; classification; assignment of call numbers

.5   Services to users

.6	**Circulation services**
.7	**Physical preparation for storage**
	Including repair and restoration
.8	**Maintenance and preservation of collections**
	Including taking of inventory, conservation
027	**General libraries, archives**
	Class here comprehensive works on libraries
.4	**Public libraries**
.6	**Libraries for special groups and organizations**
	Class here works related to church libraries
.7	**College and university libraries**
.8	**School libraries**
028	**Reading and use of other information media**
	Reading interests and habits, use of books and other media as sources of recreation and self-development
.1	**Reviews**
	General collections of book reviews
.5	**Reading and use of other information media by children and young adults**
.7	**Use of books and other media as sources of information**
	Class here use of reference works

030   General encyclopedic works

Class here general works about curiosities, books of miscellaneous facts (including almanacs), encyclopedia yearbooks

031   **American English-language general encyclopedic works**

Works originating in Western Hemisphere and Hawaii

060   General organizations

Groups whose activity is not limited to a specific field

.4   **General rules of order (Parliamentary procedure)**

069   **Museum science**

070   **Documentary media, educational media, news media; journalism; publishing**

.4   **Journalism**

100 Philosophy, parapsychology and occultism, psychology

110 Metaphysics

115 Time

116 Change

120 Causation, humankind

128 Humankind

Class here human life

Including appetite, imagination, memory, reason, will; death; human action, experience; mind, mind-body relationship; soul

130 Paranormal phenomena

133 Occultism

.4 Demonology and witchcraft

Class here the black arts including demoniac possession, evil spirits, exorcism, magic, Satanism (devil worship), spells and charms

.5 Astrology

150 Psychology

152 Sensory perception, movement, emotions, physiological drives

.1 Sensory perception

Including senses of hearing, smell, taste, touch; pain

.14 Visual perception

Including color, movement, pattern, spatial perception, optical illusions

.3 Movements and motor functions

Including coordination, reflexes

Class here comprehensive works on habits

.4 Emotions and feelings

Use for anger, aggressive moods and feelings, embarrassment, envy, fear, guilt, love and affection

Class here attitudes, moods, complexes of emotions and feelings

(Class bereavement, loneliness in 155.9, depression in 616.85)

153   **Conscious mental processes and intelligence**

        Class here intellectual processes

.1   **Memory and learning**

.2   **Formation and association of ideas**

.3   **Imagination and imagery**

        Including creativity

.4   **Knowledge (Cognition)**

        Including intuition, judgment, problem solving, reasoning, thought and thinking, value

.6   **Communication**

        Including listening; nonverbal communication (body language)

.7   **Perceptual processes**

        Understanding; perception of space, time, rhythm, movement

.8   **Will (Volition)**

        Including brainwashing, choice, decision, modification of will, persuasion, self-control; motivation

.9   **Intelligence and aptitudes**

        Including aptitude, intelligence, vocational interest tests and testing

154   **Subconscious and altered states and processes**

.6   **Sleep phenomena**

        Example: dreams

155   **Differential and developmental psychology**

.2   **Individual psychology**

        Including personality traits; development and modification of personality

.3   **Psychology of the sexes**

        Including masculinity, femininity; sex and personality; sex differences; sexual relations

.4   **Child psychology**

        Through age eleven

.44   Children by status, type, relationships

        Adopted children, twins, siblings

.5   **Psychology of young adults**

        Aged twelve to twenty

.6   **Psychology of adults**

.67   Persons in late adulthood

.9   **Environmental psychology**

Influence and effects of physical and social environments

Including influence and effect of clothing; of community and housing; of deformities, injuries, diseases; of specific situations such as accidents, disasters, death and dying, reaction to death of others; stress; bereavement; loneliness

158 **Applied psychology**

Including cooperation and negotiation, counseling and interviewing, interpersonal relations, leadership, personal improvement and analysis

.6   **Vocational interests**

.7   **Industrial psychology**

Class here psychology of work; including job stress, job burnout

170   Ethics (Moral philosophy)

174 **Economic, professional, occupational ethics**

Including medical ethics; ethics of gambling business, genetic engineering, human experimentation, industrial espionage

Class here ethics of work

175 **Ethics of recreation and leisure**

Including betting, human and animal combat, hunting, racing, theatrical performances

Class here sportsmanship, fair play

176 **Ethics of sex and reproduction**

Including artificial insemination, celibacy, contraception, homosexuality, extramarital relations, promiscuity, prostitution

177 **Ethics of social relations**

Contains benevolence, charity, conversation, courtesy, courtship, flattery, friendship, gossip, hospitality, kindness, love, lying, personal appearance

178 **Ethics of consumption**

Examples: abstinence, gluttony, greediness, overindulgence, temperance

Class here ethics of use of natural resources, of wealth

179   Other ethical norms

Including euthanasia, abortion, capital punishment, genocide, other issues concerning respect for human life; environmental ethics; courage, cowardice; profanity; respect for life and nature; treatment of children, of animals

Class here cruelty

200   Religion

Relates to the broad term "religion" or that which involves belief and worship of deity, but not necessarily God and usually not Christianity unless it is the broadest or most comprehensive use of the term.

[Comprehensive works on Christianity relocated to 230]

.1   **Philosophy and theory of religion**

[Relocated to 210]

201   **Philosophy and theory of Christianity** [Relocated to 230.01]

207   **Education, research, related topics of Christianity**

Class here Christianity as an academic subject [Relocated to 230.007]

.1   **Schools and courses** **Education**

Class theological seminaries here [Relocated to 230.071]

209   **Historical, geographical, persons treatment of Christianity and Christian thought** [Relocated to 270]

210   Natural theology

Changed to Philosophy and theory of religion

Religious beliefs and attitudes attained through observation and interpretation of evidence in nature, through speculation, through reasoning, but not through revelation (relates to a philosophical concept of the topics covered rather than to a Christian application)

211   **Concepts of God**

Do not use for a Christian concept of God

.6   **Humanism and secularism**

.7   **Agnosticism and skepticism**

.8   **Atheism**

218   **Humankind**

Including immortality

220   Bible

Use for general works which relate to the entire Bible

.02   Bible handbooks

.07	Class here study and teaching
.076	Review and exercise
	Class here questions and answers; quizzes
.09	General historical and geographical treatment of the Bible

.1 Origins and authenticity

.13	Inspiration
	Including the authority of the Bible and biblical inerrancy
.15	Biblical prophecy and prophecies

.3 Dictionaries, encyclopedias, concordances

Class here all encyclopedias, dictionaries, and concordances related to the whole Bible or to portions of both the Old and New Testaments.

(Use 221.3 for encyclopedias, dictionaries, and concordances of the Old Testament or any of its parts and 225.3 for those related to the New Testament or any of its parts.)

.4 Original texts, early versions, early translations

.44	Hebrew
.48	Greek

.5 Modern versions and translations

.52	Specific English and Anglo-Saxon versions

Note: Church libraries may choose to create a three-line call number to separate versions on the shelf. For example the call number for a King James version would be 220.52 Bib KJV or a New American Standard version would be 220.52 Bib NASV

.53-.59   In other languages

For example:
220.531	German Bible
220.541	French Bible
220.551	Italian Bible
220.561	Spanish Bible
220.569	Portuguese Bible
220.5917	Russian Bible
220.5951	Chinese Bible
220.5956	Japanese Bible
220.5957	Korean Bible
220.596	Bible in African languages
220.597	Bible in North American native languages
220.598	Bible in South American native languages

.6 Interpretation and criticism

.7   **Commentaries**

> Class here commentaries on the entire Bible or on parts of both the Old Testament and New Testament.
>
> Class commentaries on the Old Testament in 221.7 and commentaries on the New Testament 225.7.
>
> Class commentaries on specific books or portions of the Bible with the book or portion, e.g., a commentary on the book of Ruth, 222.35, and a commentary on the Gospels, 226. Further subdivisions of these numbers are not needed for commentaries.

.8   **Nonreligious subjects treated in the Bible**

> Class here materials dealing with such topics as trees, flowers, and animals found in the Bible.

.9   **Geography, history, chronology, persons of Bible lands in Bible times**

.91   Geography

> Include here social life and customs in Bible times. Covered are subjects such as food, housing, clothing, interpersonal relationships, and business dealings in Bible times.

.92   Collected persons

> Place here collective biography of persons from both the Old Testament and New Testament. For example, a biography which is about a person from the Old Testament and a person from the New Testament would require this broader number. Complete the call number by using the first three letters of the last name of the author, editor, or compiler.
>
> Class individual and collective (when all persons are from the same Testament) biographies with the Testament in which the persons are found, e.g. Old Testament persons in 221.92 and New Testament persons in 225.92. Stories based on Bible persons are classed in 220.95; 221.95; 225.95.

.93   Archaeology (Material remains)

.95   History

> This number is applied to a history of events in the Bible rather than a history of the Bible which is classed in 220.09

.9505   Bible stories retold

> This number may be reduced to 220.95. In most instances, the number is used with J or C books and does not need to be expanded.

221   Old Testament

.1-.8   Generalities

> The breakdowns or subdivisions .1-.8 are applied to the Old Testament number 221 in the same way as they are applied to 220; e.g., with 221.3 for a dictionary of the Old Testament and 221.7 for a commentary on the Old Testament.

.92 Persons

> Use this number for both collective and individual biographies of Old Testament persons. The classification will be the same, with the first three letters of the author's last name being used to complete the call number of a collective biography. To complete the call number of an individual biography, use the first three letters of the name of the person about whom the book is written.

.93 Archeology (Material remains)

.95 History

> This number is applied to a history of events in the Old Testament

.9505 Old Testament stories retold

> (See note at 220.9505)

> Reduce to 221.95

222   Historical books of the Old Testament

.1   Pentateuch (Torah)

.11   Genesis

.12   Exodus

.13   Leviticus

.14   Numbers

.15   Deuteronomy

.16   Ten Commandments

.2   Joshua

.3   Judges and Ruth

.32   Judges

.35   Ruth

.4   Samuel

.43   1 Samuel

.44   2 Samuel

.5   Kings

.53   1 Kings

.54   2 Kings

.6   Chronicles

.63   1 Chronicles

.64   2 Chronicles

.7	**Ezra**	
.8	**Nehemiah**	
.9	**Esther**	
223	**Poetic books of the Old Testament**	
.1	**Job**	
.2	**Psalms**	
.7	**Proverbs**	
.8	**Ecclesiastes**	
.9	**Song of Solomon**	
224	**Prophetic books of the Old Testament**	
.1	**Isaiah**	
.2	**Jeremiah**	
.3	**Lamentations**	
.4	**Ezekiel**	
.5	**Daniel**	
.6	**Hosea**	
.7	**Joel**	
.8	**Amos**	
.9	**Minor prophets**	
.91		Obadiah
.92		Jonah
.93		Micah
.94		Nahum
.95		Habakkuk
.96		Zephaniah
.97		Haggai
.98		Zechariah
.99		Malachi

225 **New Testament**

.1-.8 Generalities

> The breakdowns or subdivisions .1-.8 are applied to the New Testament number 225 in the same way as they are applied to 220; e.g., with 225.3 for a dictionary of the New Testament and 225.7 for a commentary on the New Testament.

.9 **Geography, history, chronology, persons of New Testament lands in New Testament times.**

> Class Jesus Christ, Mary, Joseph, and John the Baptist in 232.

.92 New Testament biography

> Use for both individual and collective biographies of New Testament persons except for persons listed in note under 225.9.

> *(See note under 221.92 for completing call number.)*

.95 New Testament stories retold

226 **Gospels and Acts**

.1 **Harmonies of the Gospels**

.2 **Matthew**

.3 **Mark**

.4 **Luke**

.5 **John**

.6 **Acts of the Apostles**

.7 **Miracles**

> Class miracles in the context of Jesus' life in 232.955

.8 **Parables**

> Class parables in the context of Jesus' life in 232.954

.9 **Sermon on the Mount**

.93 Beatitudes

.96 Lord's Prayer

227 **Epistles**

.1 **Romans**

.2 **1 Corinthians**

.3 **2 Corinthians**

.4 **Galatians**

.5 **Ephesians**

.6	**Philippians**
.7	**Colossians**
.8	**Other Pauline epistles**
.81	1 Thessalonians
.82	2 Thessalonians
.83	1 Timothy
.84	2 Timothy
.85	Titus
.86	Philemon
.87	Hebrews
.9	**Catholic epistles**
.91	James
.92	1 Peter
.93	2 Peter
.94	1 John
.95	2 John
.96	3 John
.97	Jude
228	**Revelation**
229	**Apocrypha, pseudepigrapha, intertestamental works**

This section is for books considered by some as sacred Christian writing but not included in most Christian Bibles.

230-280 Christianity

>

Within these divisions are numbers which relate specifically to the Christian religion

---

230-270 Specific elements of Christianity

>

Class here specific elements of specific denominations and sects

230   Christianity   Christian theology

The word "theology" here refers to "what the Bible teaches."

Comprehensive works on Christianity relocated from 200

.03	Dictionary of doctrine

.1-.9   Doctrines of specific denominations and sects

These numbers are used for books which treat two or more doctrines of a specific denomination. A denominational or sect treatment of a specific doctrine is classed with the subject, e.g., Methodist doctrine about the goodness of God, 231.8. The numbers 281-289 are for specific denominations and sects. If doctrines are included with other information about the denomination, class the book with the aspect which predominates. Otherwise, the 280s are preferred for denominational treatments.

.2	**Roman Catholic doctrines**
.41	Lutheran doctrines
.5	**Presbyterian doctrines**
.6	**Baptist doctrines**
.7	**Methodist doctrines**

230.01	Philosophy and theory of Christianity [Relocated from 201]
230.007	Education, research, related topics of Christianity [Relocated from 207]
230.071	Education, including theological seminaries [Relocated from 207.1]

> 231-236 Specific topics in Christian doctrinal theology

Class comprehensive works in 230

231   God

Include the "death of God" controversy here

.044	Class here comprehensive works on the Holy Trinity
.1	**God the Father**
.2	**God the Son**
.3	**God the Holy Spirit**
.4	**Attributes**

Examples: omnipotence, omnipresence

.5	**Providence**

Includes the will of God

.6	**Love and wisdom**
.7	**Relation to the world**

Examples: relation to nature, sovereignty

Class here God's relation to individual believers

.72	Kingdom of God

Class the Kingdom of God to come in 236

.73 Miracles

Class miracles of Jesus in 232.955

.74 Revelation

Vision and appearing of God, disclosure to men of divine purpose and superhuman knowledge

.76 Relation to and action in history

Examples: covenant relationship

.765 Creation

.8 **Justice and goodness**

Class here God's justice and goodness in permitting existence of evil and suffering

232 Jesus Christ and his family   Christology

.1-.8 **Christology**

This section relates to Jesus Christ as Messiah, Savior, and Lord. The subjects included have implications and meaning for Christianity and its teachings. Some of the subjects also relate to chronological events in the Life of Christ. These chronological aspects are found in 232.9 and its breakdowns.

.1 **Incarnation and messiahship of Christ**

.2 **Christ as the Word of God**

.3 **Christ as Redeemer**

Including atonement

.4 **Sacrifice of Christ**

.5 **Resurrection of Christ**

.8 **Divinity and humanity of Christ**

.9 **Family and life of Jesus**

The subjects covered in this section are especially concerned with the earthly life of Jesus and the events and persons related to it.

.901 Life of Jesus

.903 Character and personality of Jesus

.904 Jesus as teacher and example

Including influence

Class teachings in 232.954

.91 Mary, mother of Jesus

.92	Infancy of Jesus
	Including nativity
.94	John the Baptist
.95	Public life of Jesus

Baptism, included here, is the actual event of the baptism of Jesus. Media on the ordinance and teachings related to baptism are located in 265.1. Media on baptism as a part of a worship service are classed in 264.9.

.954	Teachings
.955	Miracles
.956	Transfiguration
.957	Last Supper

This number is for books about the Last Supper as an event in the life of Christ, or when it actually occurred. Use 264.36 for media on the doctrine, ordinance, and observance of the Lord's Supper.

.958	Last words to disciples
.96	Passion and death of Jesus

Most titles in this section relate to the actual crucifixion and death of Jesus.

Use 232.3 for the atonement or the meaning of the death of Christ to Christianity.

.963	Crucifixion and death
.97	Resurrection, appearances, ascension of Jesus

Resurrection here refers to the actual event in the life of Christ. Teachings about the resurrection as a basic premise in Christianity are classed in 232.5, resurrection of the dead, 236.8.

233   Humankind

This term is used for materials which may be designated as "mankind."

.1   Creation and fall

.4   Accountability

Including guilt

.5   Nature

Including body, soul, spirit; as image and likeness of God, as child of God

.7   Freedom of choice between good and evil

234   Salvation and grace

.1   Kinds and means of Grace

.12	Gifts of the Holy Spirit
.13	Spiritual gifts
.16	Sacraments

> This number relates to the salvation aspects of the topic. It will not be needed in collections in most non-Catholic libraries. A discussion of the pros and cons of the practice of infant baptism is placed in 265.1.

.161	Baptism
.162	Confirmation
.163	Eucharist, Holy Communion, Lord's Supper
.164	Holy Orders
.165	Matrimony
.166	Penance

> Including confession

.167	Anointing of the sick
.2	**Faith and hope**
.3	**Redemption**
.4	**Regeneration**
.5	**Repentance and forgiveness**
.6	**Obedience**
.7	**Justification**
.8	**Sanctification and holiness**
.9	**Predestination and free will**
235	**Spiritual beings**
.2	**Saints**

> Including beatification and canonization

.3	**Celestial hierarchy**

> Examples: angels, archangels, cherubim, seraphim

.4	**Devils (Demons)**

> Here are doctrinal or biblical-related teachings on demons. Media on demonology or demons as a part of the occult are classed in 133.4.

.47	Satan

236   Eschatology

This subject deals with those teachings concerning "last things" or the time and events from death through the last judgment.

.1   Death

.2   Future state (Life after death)

Class resurrection of the dead in 236.8

.21   Eternity

.22   Immortality

.24   Heaven

.25   Hell

.5   Purgatory

.8   Resurrection of the dead

.9   Last judgment and related events

Includes Second Coming of Christ, millennium, Armageddon, rapture, tribulation

238   Creeds, confessions of faith, covenants, catechisms

239   Apologetics

Defenses of Christianity against teachings of other religions are included here.

240   Christian moral and devotional theology

This division relates to the application of Christian teachings and the moral concepts of Christianity. Use 240 for a book of a general devotional nature in which the entire book is a continuous treatment or study in continuity and needs to be used in its entirety for full impact. If a book is divided into chapters which may be used or studied at random and is of a devotional nature, class it in 242. Devotional-type material about a specific subject, such as prayer, is classed with the subject. Class devotional literature for specific times, occasions, consolation, and specific classes of people in subdivisions of 242.

241   Moral theology

.1   Conscience

.3   Sin and vices

Include here pride, anger, covetousness, lust, envy, sloth, and gluttony

.4   Virtues

Include here love, faith, hope, fortitude, temperance, justice, and prudence as Christian virtues.

.5   Codes of conduct

.6		**Specific moral issues**
.62		Morality of warfare
.63		Ethics of divorce
.64		Questions of life and death
.66		Sexual ethics
.69		Morality of abortion

242 Devotional Literature

Class here texts of meditations, contemplations, prayers for individuals and families, religious poetry intended for devotional use.

.2   **Prayers and meditations for daily use**

.3   **Prayers and meditations for the church year**

.33   Advent and Christmas

.34   Lent

.35   Holy Week

.36   Easter

.4   **Prayers and meditations for use in time of illness, trouble, and bereavement.**

Books of a devotional nature for persons in these situations are classed here while those with more guidance in dealing with illness, trouble, and bereavement are classed in 248.86. Class books related to a specific disease with the disease. Class other books on death with the aspect of the subject with which they deal: e.g., Christian teachings on death, 236.1; the effect of death on the family, 306.88; death and burial customs, 393; philosophical approaches to death, 128; and the psychology of death, 155.9

.5   **Prayers and meditations based on passages from the Bible**

.6   **Prayers and meditations for specific classes of persons**

.62   Children

.63   Young adults

.634   College students

.64   Adults

.642   Men

.643   Women

.65   Persons in late adulthood

.7   **Specific prayers and groups of prayers**

.8   **Collections of prayers**

243   **Evangelistic writings for individuals and families.**

Class here books designed to explain the plan of salvation to a non-Christian.

245   **Texts of hymns**

Class here books which give only the words of hymns and books giving the stories of hymns

Relocated to 264.23 in latest edition of Dewey

246   **Use of art in Christianity**

Religious meaning, significance, purpose

247   **Church furnishings and related articles**

Examples: sculpture, structural decoration, paintings, textiles, plastic arts

  .1   **Furniture**

248   **Christian experience, practice, life**

(In most church libraries, this section contains a large number of titles.)

  .2   **Religious experience**

Class here conversion

  .29   Other

Class here speaking in tongues (glossolalia)

  .3   **Worship**

Include here books on the value and place of worship, prayer, meditation, and contemplation in the Christian life and books on the methods of each.

Class texts of prayers and devotions in 242.

  .4   **Christian life and practice**

Class here books which help the Christian know how to live a Christian life and books giving examples of Christian living. Books which give an overview of the life of individual Christians or which focus on a portion of the life of a specific Christian are classed as biography. Class Christian marriage and family in 306.8

  .5   **Witness bearing**

This number is used for books related to the importance of witnessing and how to witness. The emphasis here is on personal witnessing or the witnessing obligation of the Christian. Organized group witness or evangelism is classed in 269.

.6   **Stewardship**

Class here books on the stewardship of all of life and specific aspects of stewardship – time, money, and talents. Class church finance and budgeting in 254.8.

.8   **Guides to Christian life for specific classes of persons**

.82   Children

.83   Young adults

.834   College students

.84   Adults

.842   Men

.843   Women

.85   Persons in late adulthood

.86   Persons experiencing illness, trouble, bereavement

Class here books giving guidance for these persons and personal stories of those having gone through such experiences.

249   **Christian observances in family life**

Class books for and about family worship here. Include devotional guides prepared for family use.

> # 250-280 Christian church

This extensive section deals with the organized Christian church, its history, organization, and operation.

250   Local Christian church and Christian religious orders

251   **Preaching (Homiletics)**

Class here books giving guidance for preachers in the preparation and presentation of sermons.

252   **Texts of sermons**

Class here only collections of sermons about two or more subjects. A single sermon is classed with the subject of the sermon. A book of sermons on one subject is classed with the subject. If it is not possible to determine the subject of the sermon, class the book with the Scripture text used. For example, a book of sermons on prayer and worship in the life of a Christian is classed 248.3; a book of sermons or a single sermon with Psalm 23 as the text is classed 223.2.

.1   **For baptisms, confirmations, weddings, funerals**

.3   **For evangelistic meetings**

.5   **For specific classes of persons**

.53	Children

.6   For church and public occasions

Class here sermons for Advent, Christmas, Easter and other seasonal topics.

.7   For consecrations, ordinations, installations.

.9   For memorial occasions

253   Pastoral office and work (Pastoral theology)

Limit this number to pastors and their lives and ministries. Class books about other staff members at 254.

.2   Life and person

Including professional and personal qualifications, families of clergy

.5   Counseling and spiritual direction

.7   Pastoral methods

Including evangelistic work

254   Local church government and administration

Include here church staff members and their work.

.1   Initiation of new churches

Class here books on new churches, church starting, and church planting through local congregations and mission boards.

.2   In specific kinds of communities

.22	Urban
.23	Suburban
.24	Rural

.3   Use of communications media

Including use of audiovisual materials

.4   Public relations and publicity

.5   Membership

Promotion and growth

.6   Programs

Planning and execution

.7   Buildings, equipment, grounds

.8   Finance

255 **Religious congregations and orders**

Most non-Catholic church media libraries will not need this number or its breakdowns.

259 **Activities of the local church**

Pastoral care of families, of specific kinds of persons

Class here general books not identified with religious education (268) or missions (266).

.1 **Activities with families**

.2 **Activities with young people**

In this section the word Activities changes to Pastoral care.

.22 With children

.23 With youth

Ages twelve through seventeen

.24 With college students

.3 **Activities with persons in late adulthood**

.4 **Activities with handicapped and ill** of persons with disabilities

Class here hospital chaplaincy, programs for visiting the sick.

.5 **Activities with delinquents and criminals**

Class here pastoral methods in prisons, prison chaplaincy

.6 **Activities with the bereaved**

.8 **Specific types of activity**

Including recreational and camp programs

Class retreats in 269.6

260 Christian social and ecclesiastical theology

Institutions, services, observances, disciplines, work of Christianity and the Christian church. This division covers the Christian church as a whole, its influence, organization, services, and relationships. The administration of a local church is found in the 250s.

261 **Social theology and interreligious relations and attitudes**

Attitude of Christianity and the Christian church toward and influence on secular matters, attitude toward other religions, relations between religious groups. Include here the relationship of Christianity in the organized church to social concerns.

.1 **Role of the Christian church in society**

.2 **Christianity and other systems of belief**

.5   **Christianity and secular disciplines**

Including philosophy, logic, attitude toward and use of communications media, science, technology, medicine, art and literature.

.7   **Christianity and political affairs**

Class here Christianity and civil rights

.72   Religious freedom

.8   **Christianity and socioeconomic problems**

.83   Social problems

Including crime, social structure, relation of the sexes, ecology and population

.85   The economic order

.87   International affairs

Including war and peace, nuclear weapons, and nuclear war

262   **Ecclesiology**

Church government, organization, nature, including church polity and church renewal

.1   **Governing leaders of churches**

Including deacons, although Baptists do not identify deacons as governing leaders

.2   **Local church in church organization**

.3   **Government and organization of systems governed by papacy and episcopacy**

Examples: sees, dioceses, cathedral systems

.4   **Government and organization of systems governed by election**

Examples: congregational systems, presbyteries, synods

.5   **General councils**

Including ecumenical councils of the Roman Catholic Church

.7   **Nature of the church**

Including God's relation to the church

Class here the doctrine of the church, including the autonomy of the local church and the doctrine of church membership

263   **Days, times, places of religious observance**

.4   **Sunday observance**

.9   **Church year and other days and times**

.91	Advent and Christmas
.93	Easter

264   Public worship

Ceremonies, rites, services (liturgy and ritual)

Include books about the value of and need for public worship as well as those related to the components of a worship service.

.1   Prayer

Use this number as it relates to the inclusion and place of prayer in public worship. Use 264.13 for books of prayers for public worship or prayers which have been used in public worship. Class private prayer in the life of the Christian in 248.3

| .13 | Prayers used in public worship |

.2   Music

Class here comprehensive works on texts of hymns

| .23 | Text of hymns for devotional use of individuals and families |

.3   Scripture reading and communion sacrament

| .36 | Eucharist, Holy Communion, Lord's Supper, Mass |

Class here books on the Lord's Supper as a church ordinance and as a part of a worship service. Books on the Last Supper as an event in the life of Christ are classed in 232.957

.4   Responsive readings

.5   Confessions of faith

.6   Sermons, exhortations, instructions

Class here the invitation period of a worship service

.7   Prayer meetings

Include prayer groups

.9   Sacramentals

Baptism as it relates to the actual worship service is placed here. Books on baptism as a church ordinance and its Christian meaning are classed in 265.1

265   Sacraments, other rites and acts

.1   Baptism

Class here media on the meaning and doctrine of baptism. Media on the observance of baptism as a part of a worship service are classed in 264.9. Media on the baptism of Jesus are classed in 232.95

.5   Matrimony

.8   **Rites in illness and death**

Include the Christian funeral

266   Missions

Include the history of missions

.02   Kinds of missions

.022   Home missions

Class here media about home missions as a whole or any aspect of home missions.

.023   Foreign missions

Class here media about foreign missions as a whole or aspects of foreign missions, except medical missions.

.025   Medical missions

Use this number for medical missions as a whole or any aspect of medical missions. Class media about medical missionaries or about a specific medical missionary in 266.092.

.06   Missionary societies

Include here titles related to missions organizations, programs, and auxiliaries. Class missions programs for men and boys in 267.2

.073   Students, learners, apprentices, novices

Class here the call and training of career missionaries and volunteers. Include special programs for volunteers and short-term service in either home or foreign missions.

.09   Missionary stories

Use for fictional stories with a missions setting or designed to teach missions facts or concepts. Class stories containing extensive factual information about a particular type of mission work or missions in a specific place with the subject. Media classed here will be J or C. Class fictional titles for adults as fiction.

.092   Missionary biography

Class here media about individual missionaries or groups of missionaries when the emphasis is on the person(s) included. When the emphasis is on the kind or place, classify with that type or location.

Note: Complete the call number for a missionary biography by using the first three letters of the missionary's last name rather than the author's last name. For a collective biography use the first three letters of the last name of the author, compiler, or editor.

266.4-266.9 Treatment by continent, country, locality.

> For most church libraries missions materials may be classified as home or foreign missions plus a Sears Subject Heading for the specific location. However, materials may be classified geographically by applying the following numbers for a more specific location:

266.4 Missions in Europe

266.5 Missions in Asia

.51 China

.52 Japan

.54 India

266.6 Missions in Africa

266.7 Missions in North America

266.8 Missions in South America

266.9 Missions in other parts of the world including the Pacific Ocean islands

267 Associations for religious work

.1 Of both men and women

.2 Of men

> Baptists will use this number for missions programs for men and boys.

.4 Of women

> Class here Christian women's groups other than missions organizations which will be classed in 266.06.

.6 Of young adults

> Class here media about the Baptist Student Union. Missions organizations for young women will be classed in 266.06.

.7 Of boys

> Class missions programs for boys in 267.2; missions programs for young children in 266.06.

.8 Of girls

> Class missions programs for girls and young children in 266.06.

268 Religious Education (Sunday School and other organizations for training and Christian discipleship)

.1 Administration

.2 Buildings and equipment

.3 **Personnel**

Class here preparation, role, training, personnel management

.4 **Religious education of specific groups**

Class here curriculums, records and rules, teaching methods, services for specific groups. Class Vacation Bible School here as well as special ministries to the homebound

.43 Specific age groups

.432 Children

Through age twelve (Include both preschool and children's divisions)

.433 Young people

Youth Division (ages 12-17)

.434 Adults

Ages 18 and up

.5 **Records and rules**

Including attendance, decorations, honor rolls, prizes, promotion

.6 **Methods of instruction and study**

Use this number for curriculums

.61 Including Sunday School lesson commentaries

.632 Lecture method

Including storytelling. Class comprehensive works on storytelling in 808.5

.635 Audiovisual methods

.7 **Services**

Including anniversaries, festivals, music, order of service, rallies, special days, installation services

Class services for special groups in 268.4

Include here books containing planned worship programs for religious education groups, books about planned worship programs, and miscellaneous collections of materials specifically designed for worship programs.

Class brief sermons for children in 252.53. Class church worship in 264.

269 **Spiritual Renewal**

Class here books on organized evangelistic work and outreach. Class personal outreach or witnessing in 248.5, church renewal in 262.

.2   **Evangelism**

> Class here comprehensive works on evangelism
>
> Class evangelistic writings for individuals and families in 243, witness bearing by individual lay Christians in 248.5, texts of evangelistic sermons in 252.3, missionary evangelization in 266, pastoral evangelism in 253.7

.24   Revival and camp meetings

.26   Evangelism by radio and television

.6   **Retreats**

270   Historical, geographical, persons treatment of organized Christian church (Church history)

> This division covers all historical aspects of the Christian church as a whole. The emphasis here is Christianity organized into churches and not the denomination. The history of a specific denomination or sect is placed in the 280s with the denomination or sect.

.072   Research

> Including guidance in the writing of church history

.1   **Apostolic period to 325 (early church)**

.6   **Reformation, 1517-1648**

.8   **Modern period, 1789-**

.82   Twentieth century, 1900

271   **Religious congregations and orders in church history**

272   **Persecutions in general church history**

273   **Doctrinal controversies and heresies in general church history**

>   274-279   Treatment by continent, country, locality

> These numbers are for media with a historical or geographical treatment of organized Christianity or the organized church in a specific location.

274   **Christian church in Europe**

275   **Christian church in Asia**

276   **Christian church in Africa**

277   **Christian church in North America**

278   **Christian church in South America**

279   **Christian church in other parts of the world**

280 Christian Denominations and Sects

Numbers in this division are used for media about specific denominations and sects. Place here historical and geographical works and comprehensive treatments of the subject(s). Surveys and overviews of the groups are also included. Class doctrines of a specific denomination in 230.1–.9.

.042   Relations between denominations

281 Early church and Eastern churches

282 Roman Catholic Church

Place here media dealing with the Roman Catholic Church from a comprehensive view or a general treatment of the subject.

> 283-289 Protestant and other denominations

283 Anglican churches

284 Protestant denominations of Continental origin and related bodies

.1   **Lutheran churches**

.6   **Moravian churches**

285 Presbyterian churches, Reformed churches centered in America, Congregational churches

286 Baptist, Disciples of Christ, Adventist churches

Use this number for a comprehensive treatment of this group of churches. The number for Southern Baptist Convention (286.132) may be shortened to this number as well in most local church collections. This number also includes the local Baptist association and its work.

.03   Use for an encyclopedia of Baptists

.06   Use for proceedings and reports such as convention annuals

.09   History

Use for a history of Baptists or a history of the Southern Baptist Convention

.092   Baptist biography

.1   **Regular Baptists**

.132   Southern Baptist Convention

.2   **Freewill Baptists**

.3   **Seventh-Day Baptists**

.4   **Old School Baptists**

> Including Hard-Shell and Primitive

.5   **Other Baptist churches and denominations**

> Including General Baptists and Church of the Brethren

.6   **Disciples of Christ (Campbellites)**

.7   **Adventist churches**

287   **Methodist churches, churches uniting Methodists and other denominations, Salvation Army**

.1   **Wesleyan Methodist Church**

.2   **Miscellaneous Methodist churches**

.4   **Primitive Methodist Church**

.5   **Methodist churches in the British Isles**

.6   **United Methodist Church**

.7   **Methodist Protestant Church**

.8   **Black Methodist churches of United States origin**

.9   **Churches uniting Methodist and other denominations**

.96   Salvation army

289   **Other denominations and sects**

.1   **Unitarian and Universalist churches**

.3   **Latter-Day Saints (Mormons)**

.5   **Church of Christ, Scientist (Christian Science)**

.6   **Society of Friends (Quakers)**

.7   **Mennonite churches**

.8   **Shakers**

.9   **Others**

> Include here Church of the Nazarene, Churches of God, Jehovah's Witnesses, Pentecostal churches such as Assemblies of God, United Pentecostal Church, and independent fundamentalist and evangelical churches

290   Comparative religions and religions other than Christianity

291   **Comparative religions**

> Use this number for media which compare various aspects of two or more religions.

.2   **Doctrines**

300   Social sciences

301   Sociology and anthropology

Include interdisciplinary works on society

302   Social interaction

Including cooperation, competition; social dysfunctions

Class here social psychology

.2   **Communication**

Including body language, rumor

.23   Media (means of communication)

.3   **Social interaction within groups**

Including bureaucracy, committees, conversation, gangs, mobs

.4   **Social interaction between groups**

.5   **Relation of the individual to society**

Including ambition, individualism, alienation, aggression

303   Social processes

.3   **Coordination and control**

Including censorship, coercion, leadership, prejudice, persuasion, propaganda, public opinion, values

.4   **Social change**

.48   Causes of change

.6   **Conflict**

Including civil disobedience, war

304   Factors affecting social behavior

.6   **Population**

Population size and composition of communities relocated from 307.2

305   Social groups

Including social status

.2   **Age groups**

Class here generation gap

.23	Young people
	Through age 20
	Including child development
.24	Adults
.26	Late adulthood
.3	**Men and women**
.31	Men
.32	Social role and status of men
.33	Men's occupations
.38	Specific kinds of men
	Include single men; widowers
.4	**Women**
.42	Social role and status of women
.43	Women's occupations
.48	Specific kinds of women
	Include single women; widows
.5	**Social classes**
	Upper, middle, lower classes; white-collar, poor, homeless
.7	**Language groups**
.8	**Racial, ethnic, national groups**
	Class here ethnology, race relations, race discrimination
.9	**Occupational and miscellaneous groups**
306	**Culture and institutions**
.2	**Political institutions**
.3	**Economic institutions**
	Including retirement
.43	Educational sociology, moved from 370
.7	**Institutions pertaining to relations of the sexes**
.73	General sexual relations
	Including celibacy, courtship, premarital sexual relations, adultery, extramarital relations
	Class here dating

310   General statistics

Collections of quantitative data

320   Political science (Politics and government)

322   Relation of the state to organized groups and their members

323   Civil and political rights

Class here relation of the state to its residents; individual freedom, human rights, rights of mankind

324   The political process

Class here elections

326   Slavery and emancipation

Class interdisciplinary works on slavery in 306.3

330   Economics

331   Labor economics

.1   **Labor force and market**

.2   **Compensation and other conditions of employment**

.3   **Workers of specific age groups**

.4   **Women workers**

.7   **Labor by industry and occupation**

Interdisciplinary works on career opportunities and vocational counseling

332   Financial economics

.024   Personal finance

Including increasing income, planning for retirement, estate planning, debt management

.4   **Money**

.6   **Investment and investments**

Including investment counselors

.7   **Credit**

Including real estate finance and mortgages, small business loans, personal loans, consumer credit, bankruptcy, credit cards

333   Land economics   Economics of land and energy

.7   **Natural resources and energy**

Interdisciplinary works on the environment

.79		Energy
		Including energy conservation

336   **Public finance**

.2   **Taxes and taxation**

338   **Production**

       Including production efficiency

.1   **Agriculture**

340   Law

.5   **Legal systems**

342   **Constitutional and administrative law**

       Including civil service

.73   Constitutional law of United States

348   **Laws (Statutes), regulations, cases**

       Including codes, digests

349   **Law of specific jurisdictions**

360   Social problems and services; association

361   **Social problems and social welfare in general**

.1   **Social problems**

.2   **Social action**

.3   **Social work**

.6   **Governmental action**

       Including welfare and human rights

.7   **Private action**

       By individual philanthropists, by religious organization; by other nonprofit organizations, including Red Cross

.8   **Community action**

       Coordination of public and private action to promote welfare of individuals in the community

362   **Social welfare problems and services**

       Class here social security

.1   **Physical illness**

       Including living with a physical illness

.3   **Offenders**

Including juvenile delinquents

.4   **Prevention of crime and delinquency**

Including counseling and guidance

368   **Insurance**

369   **Miscellaneous kinds of associations**

Including scouting

370   Education

Educational sociology moved to 306.43

371   **School organization and management; special education**

.042   Home schools, relocated from 649

.07   Religious schools, relocated from 377

.1   **Teaching and teaching personnel**

Including the relation of teachers to society, for example parent-teacher relations; teaching methods; classroom discipline

.2   **School administration and management**

Including tuition in private schools; accreditation; grouping of pupils for instructions; promotion and failure; scholarships; school dropouts, truancy

.3   **Methods of instruction and study**

Including use of audio and visual materials, print media

.4   **Guidance and counseling**

Educational, vocational, personal

Class choice of vocation in 331.7

.5   **School discipline**

Overseeing student conduct; student government

Class classroom discipline in 371.1

.6   **Physical plant**

Buildings; grounds

.7   **School health and safety**

Including school lunch programs

.8   **The student**

Including student activities, organizations

.9 **Special education**

Education for students with physical, intellectual, mental or social differences

372 **Elementary education**

Class here preschool education

.1 **Organization and management of elementary schools; curriculum**

.2 **Levels of elementary education**

For example nursery school, kindergarten

Class here headstart programs

.3 **Technology, science, health**

Including computers, food, hygiene, nutrition

.4 **Reading**

Including methods of instruction, for example phonics; remedial reading

.5 **Creative and manual arts**

Including design, drawing, handicrafts, modeling, sculpting, sewing

.6 **Language, literature, theater**

Class here language arts

.7 **Mathematics**

.8 **Other studies**

Including home economics, religion, physical education, music and history

.9 **Historical, geographic, persons treatment of elementary education**

373 **Secondary education**

374 **Adult education**

377 **Schools and religion**

Including religious instruction and exercises in public and other nonsectarian schools
[Relocated to 371.07]

378 **Higher education**

.3 **Student finances**

380 **Commerce, communications, transportation**

381 **Internal commerce**

Retail and wholesale trade

.3 **Commercial policy**

Consumerism

383   **Postal communication**

384   **Communications Telecommunication**

   .3   **Computer communication**

   .5   **Wireless communication**

   .54   Radiobroadcasting

   .55   Television

   .6   **Telephone**

385   **Railroad transportation**

386   **Inland waterway and ferry transportation**

387   **Water, air, space transportation**

   .2   **Ships**

   .7   **Air transportation**

   .8   **Space transportation**

388   **Transportation Ground transportation**

   .1   **Roads and highways**

   .3   **Vehicular transportation**

389   **Metrology and standardization**

        Metrology: social use of systems of measurement

        Including time systems and standards, such as daylight savings time; metric system

390   Customs, etiquette, folklore

        Class here folkways

391   **Costume and personal appearance**

        Including hair styles, body types, use of cosmetics, personal hygiene, jewelry

        Interdisciplinary works on costume, clothing, fashion

392   **Customs of life cycle and domestic life**

        Customs connected with birth, child rearing, courtship, weddings, marriage

393   **Death customs**

        Including burial, mourning

394   **General customs**

   .1   **Eating, drinking; using drugs**

.2 **Special occasions**

Including birthdays and anniversaries, festivals, and holidays

395 Etiquette (Manners)

Prescriptive and practical works on social behavior

Including hospitality and entertainment, social correspondence

398 Folklore

.6 **Riddles**

.8 **Rhymes and rhyming games**

400

400 Language

410 Linguistics

411 Writing systems

> Include here alphabets, abbreviations

412 Etymology

> History of word meanings

413 Dictionaries

> Include here specialized dictionaries, e.g., dictionaries of abbreviations
>
> Class dictionaries for specific languages with the number for the language, for example a dictionary of the English language in 423.

418 Standard usage   Applied linguistics

> Including interpretation, translation; reading

419 Structured verbal language other than spoken and written

> Class here manual language for the deaf

> ## 420-490 Specific languages

420 English

421 Guides to pronunciation

423 English dictionaries

425 Grammar

428 Standard usage

> Including basic English for persons learning English as a second language
> The following numbers for individual languages may be divided by taking the number which follows 42 in the list above for English and attaching it to the first two numbers for any language listed below. For example a grammar of the German language is 435.

430 German

440 French

450 Italian, Romanian

460 Spanish, Portuguese

470   **Latin**

480   **Greek**

490   **Other languages**

500   Natural sciences and mathematics

508   **Natural history**

        Including seasons

        New number for seasons is 508.2

510   Mathematics
520   Astronomy and allied sciences

521   **Celestial mechanics**

        Including gravity

523   **Specific celestial bodies**

   .1   **Space and the universe**

   .2   **Solar system**

   .3   **Moon**

   .4   **Planet**

   .5   **Meteoroids**

   .6   **Comets**

   .7   **Sun**

   .8   **Stars**

   .9   **Satellites and rings, eclipses**

525   **Earth**

        Astronomical aspects

526   **Mathematical geography**

        Class here map making

   .9   **Surveying**

529   **Chronology**

        Including calendars, intervals of time

530   Physics

534   **Sound and related vibrations**

535   **Light and related radiations**

567 **Fossil cold-blooded vertebrates**

    Including amphibians

    Class here fish

  .9 **Reptiles**

    Including dinosaurs

570 Life sciences

572 **Human races**

    Including causes of physical differences

574 **Biology**

  .1 **Physiology**

    Class here comprehensive works on anatomy, physiology

  .2 **Pathology**

    Including immunity

  .3 **Development and maturation**

    Including aging

  .5 **Ecology**

    Including food chains, rare and endangered species; specific kinds of environments, e.g., forests, oceans, seashores, tropics

575 **Evolution and genetics**

580 Botanical sciences Plants

581 **Botany**

  .1 **Physiology of plants**

    Including agricultural plants

582 **Seed-bearing plants**

586 **Seedless plants**

590 Zoological sciences Animals

591 **Zoology**

594 **Mollusks and mollusk-like animals**

    Examples: clams, octopuses, oysters, snails

595 **Other invertebrates**

  .1 **Worms and related animals**

.3	**Crustaceans**	
	Crabs, lobsters, shrimp	
.4	**Arachnids**	
	Including spiders	
.7	**Insects**	

597   Cold-blooded vertebrates

Class here fish

.6	**Amphibians**	
	Such as salamanders	
.8	**Anura**	
	Frogs and toads	
.9	**Reptiles**	
.92	Turtles	
.95	Lizards	
.96	Snakes	
.98	Crocodiles and alligators	

598   Birds

599   Mammals

Class here warm-blooded vertebrates

600

600 Technology (Applied sciences)

608 Inventions and patents

610 Medical sciences Medicine

.7 Education, nursing, related topics

Nursing and services of medical technicians

612 Human physiology

Class here comprehensive works on human anatomy and physiology

.1 Blood and circulation

.2 Respiration

.3 Digestion

.6 Reproduction, development, maturation

Including puberty, menopause, aging

.7 Motor functions and skin, hair, nails

Including bones, joints, muscles; exercise; voice and speech

.8 Nervous functions Sensory functions

Including brain, nerves; ears, eyes; hearing, smell, taste, touch, vision; sleep

613 Promotion of health

.2 Dietetics

Including weight gain and loss programs

Number expanded to include applied nutrition, formerly 641.1

.6 Special topics

Self defense, survival in accidents

Class here personal safety

.7 Physical fitness

Including exercise, posture, rest, sleep

.8 Substance abuse (Drug abuse)

.81 Alcohol

.85 Tobacco

.9 Birth control and sex hygiene

615   Pharmacology and therapeutics

.5   **Therapeutics**

Including drug therapy, chemotherapy

.8   **Specific therapies and kinds of therapies**

Including occupational therapy and physical therapy

.9   **Toxicology**

Including prevention, diagnosis, treatment of poisoning

Class here poisons and poisoning

616   Diseases

Class here internal medicine

.02   First aid

.1   **Diseases of the cardiovascular system**

.2   **Diseases of the respiratory system**

.5   **Diseases of the skin, hair, nails**

Class here dermatology

.7   **Diseases of the musculoskeletal system**

Including arthritis

Includes nonsurgical aspects of and comprehensive works on orthopedics

.8   **Diseases of the nervous system and mental disorders**

.85   Disorders of personality and intellect, speech and language disorders

Including amnesia, depression, learning disabilities, anorexia nervosa

.86   Substance abuse (Drug abuse)

Class here addiction

.89   Mental disorders

Class here abnormal psychology

.9   **Other diseases**

.97   AIDS, allergies

.99   Cancer

617   Miscellaneous branches of medicine   Surgery

.1   **Wounds and injuries**

.2   **Results of injuries**

   Shock

.6   **Dentistry**

618   **Other branches of medicine   Gynecology and obstetrics**

.1   **Gynecology**

   Including infertility

.2   **Obstetrics**

   Including prenatal care

.3   **Diseases and complications of pregnancy**

   Including miscarriage

.4   **Childbirth**

.9   **Pediatrics and geriatrics**

.92   Pediatrics

   Diseases of infants and children up to puberty

.97   Geriatrics

   Diseases of persons in late adulthood

620   Engineering

   Including maintenance and repair

   Class here manufacturing of products of various branches of engineering

621   **Applied physics**

.32   Lighting

.9   **Tools**

624   **Civil engineering**

   Including bridges; construction engineering

625   **Engineering of railroads, roads, highways**

   Including planning, design, construction

629   **Other branches of engineering**

.1   **Aerospace engineering**

.2   **Cars, trucks, and cycles**

.4   **Astronautics**

630   Agriculture and related technologies

Class here farming, farms, comprehensive works on plant crops

631   Specific techniques; apparatus, equipment, materials

.2   Use of agricultural structures

Such as barns, fences, roads

.3   Use of tools, machinery, apparatus, equipment

Including workshops

.4   Soil science

Including soil erosion, comprehensive works on soil and water conservation

.5   Cultivation and harvesting

.6   Clearing, drainage, revegetation

.7   Water conservation

.8   Fertilizers and soil conditioners

632   Plant injuries, diseases, pests

Including control methods, pesticides

633   Field and plantation crops

634   Orchards, fruit, forestry

635   Garden crops (Horticulture)   Vegetables

.9   Flowers and ornamental plants

Including houseplants, lawns, trees

636   Animal husbandry

.08   Veterinary sciences

.088   Pets

.1   Horses and related animals

Examples: donkeys, mules, zebras

.2   Ruminants   Bovines   Cattle

Examples: buffalo, camels, deer, llamas

Including dairy farming

.3   Sheep and goats

.4   Swine

.5   Poultry   Chickens

.6	**Birds other than poultry**	
.7	**Dogs**	
.8	**Cats**	
.9	**Other mammals**	

637   **Processing dairy and related products**

Examples: milk, butter, cheese, eggs

Including manufacture of ice cream and other frozen deserts

638   **Insect culture**

Examples: bees, silkworms

Including processing honey

639   **Hunting, fishing, conservation, related technologies**

.2   **Commercial fishing, whaling, sealing**

.3   **Culture of cold-blooded vertebrates   Of fish**

Including aquariums, fish hatcheries

.9   **Conservation of biological resources**

Class here game protection, wildlife conservation

640   Home economics and family living

Including management of household employees, of money, of time

Class here management of home and personal life, domestic arts and sciences

641   **Food and drink**

.1   **Nutrition**

Moved to 613.2

.3   **Food**

Class here interdisciplinary works on food

.5   **Cooking**

642   **Meals and table service**

Including catering, menus, picnics, table furnishings and decorations, banquets

643   **Housing and household equipment**

Including selecting, renting, buying homes; renovation, remodeling

645   Household furnishings

> Including draperies, floor coverings, furniture, lighting fixtures

646   Sewing, clothing and accessories, management of personal and family living

> Including comprehensive works on fabrics in the home

.2   Sewing and related operations

.4   Clothing and accessories construction

.7   Management of personal and family living   Grooming

> Including charm, dating, mate selection, retirement guides
>
> Class here interdisciplinary works on success, successful living

648   Housekeeping

649   Child rearing and home care of sick and infirm

> Including home schooling by parents

> Home schooling moved to 371.042

.8   Home care of sick and infirm

650   Management and auxiliary services

.1   Personal success in business

> Including financial success

.14   Success in obtaining jobs and promotions

651   Office services

.3   Office management

.7   Communication

> Including correspondence, minutes, reports

.8   Data processing   Computer applications

652   Process of written communication

.3   Typewriting

.5   Word processing

657   Accounting

658   General management

659   Advertising and public relations

> Class here publicity

660 Chemical engineering and related topics
670 Manufacturing
680 Manufacture of products for specific uses
686 Printing and related activities
690 Buildings

Planning, design, construction

694 Wood construction Carpentry

698 Detail finishing

Including carpeting, finishing woodwork, painting, paperhanging

700

700   The arts   Fine and decorative arts

701   **Art appreciation**

704   **Special topics in fine and decorative arts**

  .9   Religious symbolism

707   **Education and related topics of fine and decorative arts**

708   **Galleries, museums, private collections of art**

710   Civic and landscape art

712   **Landscape architecture (Landscape design)**

714   **Water features in landscape architecture**

715   **Woody plants in landscape architecture**

719   **Natural landscapes**

         Including forest and wildlife reserves

720   Architecture

721   **Architectural structure**

         Foundations, walls, roofs, floors, doors, windows, stairs

725   **Public structures**

726   **Buildings for religious and related purposes**

727   **Buildings for educational and research purposes**

728   **Residential and related buildings**

729   **Design and decoration of structures and accessories**

730   Plastic arts   Sculpture

736   **Carving and carvings**

         Including origami

737   **Numismatics and sigillography**

         Including buttons, medals, tokens; seals, stamps

  .4   **Coins**

738   **Ceramic arts**

         Pottery

739 **Art metalwork**

Including clocks and watches

.2 **Work in precious metals**

.27 Jewelry

.4 **Ironwork**

740 Drawing and decorative arts

741 **Drawing and drawings**

.2 **Techniques, procedures, apparatus, equipment, materials**

Charcoal, chalk, crayon, pencil; ink with pen

.5 **Cartoons, caricatures, comics**

.6 **Graphic design, illustration, and commercial art**

.7 **Silhouettes**

.9 **Collections of drawings**

745 **Decorative arts**

.1 **Antiques**

.4 **Pure and applied design and decoration**

.5 **Handicrafts**

.54 In paper

.6 **Calligraphy, illumination**

.7 **Decorative coloring**

.9 **Other decorative arts**

.92 Floral arts

Flower arrangement

746 **Textile arts and handicrafts**

.1 **Yarn preparation and weaving**

.3 **Pictures, hangings, tapestries**

.4 **Needle- and handwork**

.41 Weaving

.43 Knitting, crocheting, tatting

.44 Embroidery

.46 Patchwork and quilting

.2		**Nondramatic vocal forms**
		Including sacred vocal music
.27		Hymns
.28		Carols
.5		**Mixed voices**
.6		**Women's voices**
.7		**Children's voices**
.8		**Men's voices**

783   **Music for single voices**

784   **Instruments and instrumental ensembles and their music**

    .2   **Full (Symphony) orchestra**

    .6   **Keyboard, mechanical, electronic, percussion bands**

786   **Keyboard, mechanical, electrophonic, percussion instruments**

    .2   **Piano**

    .5   **Keyboard wind instruments   Organ**

    .7   **Electronic instruments**

        Including tape, synthesizer

    .8   **Percussion instruments**

    .9   **Drums and devices used for percussion effects**

787   **Stringed instruments**

    .2   **Violin**

788   **Wind instruments**

790   Recreational and performing arts

    .1   **Recreational activities**

        Including hobbies, collecting, play with toys

791   **Public performances**

    Other than musical, sport, game performances

    .06   Amusement parks

    .3   **Circuses**

    .4   **Motion pictures, radio, television**

.45	Television

Including use of videocassettes

.5   **Puppetry and toy theaters**

.6   **Pageantry**

.8   **Animal performances**

792   **Stage presentations**

Class here theater, dramatic presentation

793   **Indoor games and amusements**

.2   **Parties and entertainments**

.4   **Games of action**

.7   **Games not characterized by action**

.73   Puzzles and puzzle games

.8   **Magic and related activities**

Juggling, ventriloquism

794   **Indoor games of skill**

Class here board games

796   **Athletic and outdoor sports and games**

.092   Biographies of athletes; or B for single biographies

Note: For a single biography, use first three letters of last name of biographee; for collective biography use first three letters of last name of author or compiler to complete the call number.

.1   **Miscellaneous games**

.2   **Activities and games requiring equipment**

.3   **Ball games**

.4   **Weight lifting, track and field, gymnastics**

.5   **Outdoor life**

Including walking

.54   Camping

.6   **Cycling and related activities**

.9   **Ice and snow sports**

797   **Aquatic and air sports**

.1   **Boating**

.2	**Swimming and diving**
.3	**Other aquatic sports**
.5	**Air sports**
798	**Equestrian sports and animal racing**
.2	**Horsemanship**
799	**Fishing, hunting, shooting**
.1	**Fishing**
.2	**Hunting**
.3	**Shooting other than game**

Including archery

800

800   Literature and rhetoric

Class here works of literature, works about literature

808   Rhetoric and collections of literary texts from more than one literature

.5   Rhetoric of speech

Including public speaking, reading aloud, storytelling, choral speaking

Class here voice, expression, gesture

.53   Debating and public discussion

.56   Conversation

.6   Rhetoric of letters

.8   Collections of literary texts from more than one literature

By more than one author

.81   Poetry (See also 811 and 821)

.82   Plays

.88   Collections of miscellaneous writings

Including anecdotes, diaries, quotations

810   American literature in English

811   Poetry (Written in English by an American author)

812   Drama (Written in English by an American author)

813   Fiction (Written in English by an American author)

Note: In a church library classify a book of fiction as F followed by the first three letters of the author's last name.

814   Essays (Written in English by an American author)

815   Speeches (Written in English by an American author)

816   Letters (Written in English by an American author)

817   Satire and humor (Written in English by an American author)

818   Miscellaneous writings (Written in English by an American author)

820   English literature

821   English poetry

822   **English drama**

828   **English miscellany**

830   German literature
840   French literature
850   Italian literature
860   Spanish and Portuguese literature
870   Latin literature
880   Classical Greek literature
890   Literatures of other languages

900

900 Geography, history, and auxiliary disciplines

909 **World history**

910 Geography and travel

Including physical geography

.2 **Miscellany**

Including world travel guides

912 **Graphic representations of surface of earth**

Including map reading

Class here atlases, maps, charts, plans

> 913-919 Geography of and travel in ancient world and specific locations

913 **Ancient world**

914 **Europe and Western Europe**

915 **Asia   Orient   Far East**

916 **Africa**

917 **North America**

.3 **United States**

918 **South America**

919 **Other parts of world   Pacific Ocean islands**

920 Biography, genealogy, insignia

Including autobiographies, diaries, reminiscences, correspondence

Note: In a church library use B for single biographies or collective biographies from a single family. Complete the call number with the first three letters of the last name of the person or family in the biographical work. Use 920 to classify collective biographies about more than one person or family. Use the first three letters of the author's or compiler's last name to complete the call number for collective biography. See 220.92, 221.92, 225.92 and 266.092 for Bible biography and missions biography.

929 **Genealogy, names, insignia**

Including family histories; cemetery records

.4   **Personal names**

.8   **Awards, orders, decorations, autographs**

Including coats of arms, crests, seals

.9   **Forms of insignia and identification**

Flags; trademarks

> **930-990 History of ancient world and of specific locations**

930   **General history of ancient world to ca. 499**

940   **History of Europe   Western Europe**

950   **History of Asia   Orient   Far East**

960   **History of Africa**

970   **General history of North America**

971   **Canada**

972   **Middle America   Mexico**

973   **United States**

Including individual states

980   **History of South America**

990   **General history of other parts of world   Pacific Ocean islands**

Including New Zealand, Australia, New Guinea

Atlantic Ocean islands, other parts of Pacific

RELATIVE INDEX

A

Atlases	912
Atmosphere	551.5
Atonement	
Christianity	234
Attention	
psychology	
learning	153.1
Attention deficit disorder	
medicine	616.85
Attitudes	152.4
Audiovisual materials	
Christian Religious education	261.635
Australia	990
Autism	
medicine	616.89
Autobiographies	920
Autographs	929.8
Automobile accidents	363.12
Automobile driving	629.2
Automobile insurance	368
Automobile transportation	388
Automobiles	388.3
repair	629.2
Autumn	508
Aviation	387.7
technology	629.1
Awards	929.8

B

Babies	305.23
home care	649
pediatrics	618.92
Baby animals	591
Baby food	641.3
cooking	641.5
Baby sitters' handbooks	649
Bachelors	305.38
Back	
human physiology	612
Backpacking	796.5
Baking	
cooking	641
Ball games	796.3
indoor	794
outdoor	796.3

Balloons	
engineering	629.1
sports	797.5
Ballot	324
Bananas	641.3
cooking	641.5
Bandaging	
first aid	616.02
Bands	784
Banjo	787
Bank accounts	332
Banking	332
Bankruptcy	332.7
Banquets	642
Baptism	234
public worship	265.1
Baptism in the Holy Spirit	234.12
Baptists	286
biography	286.092
doctrines	230.6
Bar mitzvah	296.4
Barbering	646.7
Barns	631.2
Baseball	796.3
Basic English	428
Basketball	796.3
Basketry	
handicrafts	746.41
Bass (stringed instrument)	787
Bassoon	788
Bathing	
health	613
Beaches	551.4
Beans	641.3
agriculture	635
Bears	599
Beatitudes	226.9
Bees	595.7
processing honey	638
Beetles	595.7
Behavior	
animals	591
biology	574.5
general psychology	150
social psychology	302
Behavior modification	153.8
educational psychology	370

Broken homes	362.82
sociology	306.89
Brothers	306.875
Buddhism	294.3
Building	
technology	690
remodeling	690
Buildings	720
architecture	720
construction	690
Bulimia	
medicine	616.85
Bulletin boards	
education	371.3
Burglarproofing	
home economics	643
Burglary	364.1
see also Crime	
Burglary insurance	368
Burnout	
psychology	158.7
Burns	
medicine	617.1
Bus drivers	388
Buses	388
Business	650
Business ethics	174
Business etiquette	395
Business management	658
Business success	650.1
Butterflies	595.7
Buttons	
commercial technology	680
home sewing	646
numismatics	737
Buyers' guides	381.3
home economics	640
Bypass surgery (Coronary)	617

C

Cakes (Pastry)	641
Calculators	680
mathematics	510
Calendars	529
Calisthenics	613.7
therapeutics	615.8

Calligraphy	745.6
Calorie counters	641
Calvinistic churches	284
Cameras	770
Camp meetings	
Christian religious	
practices	269
Campaigns for election	324
Campbellites	286.6
Camping	796.54
Camping equipment	680
Canada	971
Canadians	971
civilization	971
Canals	386
Cancer	362.1
medicine	616.99
social services	362.1
Candles	621.32
Candy	641
Canoeing	
sports	797.1
Canon of Bible	220.1
Cantatas	782
Capital punishment	364
Card catalogs	025.3
Cardiovascular system	
human diseases	
medicine	616.1
human physiology	612.1
surgery	617
Career education	370
Career opportunities	331.7
Caricatures	741.5
Caring	
moral theology	
Christianity	241.4
Carnivals	
customs	394.2
Carols	782.28
Carpentry	694
Carpeting	645
Cars (Automobiles)	388
engineering	629.2
Cartography	526
Cartoons	741.5
Carving	736

Choice	
psychology	153.8
Choice of vocation	331.7
Choral music	782.5
Choral speaking	
rhetoric	808.5
Christening	265.1
Christian art	
religious significance	246
Christian Church (Disciples	
of Christ)	286.6
Christian denominations	280
Christian doctrine	230
Christian education	268
Christian ethics	241
Christian life	248.4
Christian schools	377
Christian Science	289.5
Christianity	200
Christianity and culture	261
Christianity and politics	261.7
Christianity and socioeconomic	
problems	261.8
Christmas	263.91
customs	394.2
devotional literature	242.33
Christmas carols	782.28
Chronic diseases	
medicine	616
Chronicles (Bible book)	222.6
Chronology	529
Church	262
Church and education	377
Church and state	322
Christianity	261.7
Church authority	262
Church buildings	
architecture	726
management	254.7
Church furniture	247
Church government	262
Church growth	
local	254.5
Church history	270
specific denominations	280
Church holidays	263
customs	394.2

Church libraries	027.6
Church membership	
local	254
Church music	781.7
Church of Christ,	
Scientist	289.5
Church of England	283
Church of God in Christ,	
Mennonites	289.7
Church of Jesus Christ of	
Latter-Day Saints	289.3
Church of the Nazarene	289.9
Church organization	262
Church planting	254.1
Church schools	377
Church services	264
Church work with children	259.22
Church work with college	
students	259.24
Church work with families	259.1
Church work with juvenile	
delinquents	259.5
Church work with the aged	259.3
Church work with the	
handicapped	259.4
Church work with the sick	259.4
Church work with youth	259.23
Church year	263.9
Church youth groups	259.23
Churches of Christ	286.6
Churches of God	289.9
Cigarette habit	362.29
Circulation (Biology)	574.1
Circulatory system	
human physiology	612.1
plant physiology	581.1
Circus	791.3
Cities	307.76
Citizen participation	323
Citizenship	323
City planning	307.1
Civil rights	323
law	342
Clams	594
Clarinet	788
Classroom discipline	371.1
Classroom management	371.1

D

Evangelical United Brethren Church	289.9
Evangelism	269.2
Evil (Concept)	
religion	
Christianity	230
freedom of choice	233
Evil spirits	133.4
Evolution	575
Evolution versus creation	
Christianity	231.7
Ex-convicts	364
Exceptional children	
psychology	155.4
Exceptional students	371.9
Exegesis	
Bible	220.6
Exercise	613.7
Exodus (Bible)	222.12
Expectant parents'	
handbooks	649
medicine	618.2
Extended care facilities	362.1
Eyes	591
human diseases	
medicine	617
human physiology	612.8
Ezekiel (Biblical book)	224.4
Ezra (Biblical book)	222.7

F

Fables	
folklore	398
Face	
personal care	646.7
Facsimile transmission	384
Factories	
manufacturing industries	338
Failure (Education)	371.2
Fairy tales	398
Faith	
Christianity	234
Fall	508
Families	306.85
church work with	259.1
guides to Christian living	248.4

worship	
Christianity	249
Family counseling	362.82
Family dissolution	306.88
Family histories	929
Family life	306.85
customs	392
home economics	646.7
Family medicine	610
Family names	929.4
Family planning	
health	613.9
Family relationships	306.87
Family violence	362.82
psychiatry	616.85
Famine	363.8
Farm buildings	
use	631.2
Farm machinery	631.3
Farm pests	632
Farm produce	
agricultural technology	630
Farming	630
economics	338.1
Farms	630
animal husbandry	636
resource economics	333.7
Fashion	391
Fashion design	746
Fashion drawing	741.6
Fasting	
religious practice	
Christianity	248.4
Father and child	306.874
Fatherhood	306.874
Fathers	306.874
psychology	155.6
Fatigue (Human)	
psychology	152.1
Fear	152.4
Feast days	
customs	394.2
Feelings	152.4
Feet	
human physiology	612
Felines	599

Foster children	306.874
psychology	155.4
Foster homes	362.7
Foster parents	306.874
Fountains	
landscape architecture	714
Fraud	364.1
occultism	133
Free will	
religion	
Christian	233.7
Freedom (Personal liberty)	323
Freedom of religion	323
Freedom of speech	323
law	342
Freedom of the press	323
law	342
French language	440
French literature	840
Friends (Religious society)	289.6
Friendship	
applied psychology	158
ethics	177
social psychology	302.3
Frogs	597.8
Frost	551.57
Fruit	582
orchard crop	634
Fundamentalist movement	270.8
Fundamentalist theology	230
Funerals	393
customs	393
etiquette	395
religious rites	
Christianity	265.8
Furnishings	645
interior decoration	747
Furniture	645
decorative arts	749
household management	645
Future life	
religion	
Christianity	236

G

Galatians (Biblical book)	227.4

Gambling	
ethics	175
public control	363
Games	790
indoor	793
outdoor	796
Gangs	
criminology	364.1
sociology	302.3
Garage sales	381
Garbage disposal	363
Garden furniture	645
Gardening	635
Gardens	635
landscape architecture	712
Garments	391
Gas (Natural gas)	553
Gasoline engines	621
Gays	305.9
Gem cutting	736
Gems	553
Genealogy	929
Generation gap	305.2
Genesis (Bible)	222.11
Genetic disorders	
medicine	616
Genetic engineering	
ethics	174
Genetics	575
Genius	153.9
Geography	910
Bible	220.9
Geology	551
Geriatrics	618.97
German language	430
German literature	830
Ghosts	
folklore	398
Giants	
folklore	398
Gifted children	
psychology	155
Gifted students	371.9
Gifts of the Holy Spirit	234.12
Girls	305.23
psychology	155.4
Glaciers	551.3

H

Harmony	
musical element	781.2
Harp	787
Harpsichord	786
Harvesting	631.5
Hats	391
Head	
human physiology	612
Headache	
medicine	616.8
Headstart (Education)	372
Health	613
child care	649
Health cooking	641.5
Health food	641.3
Health insurance	368
Health resorts	613
Health services	362.1
Hearing	
human physiology	612.8
psychology	152.1
Hearing aids	
audiology	617
Hearing-impaired persons	
education	371.9
social welfare	362.4
Heart	
human physiology	612.1
Heart diseases	
medicine	616
Heart surgery	617
Heat	536
Heaven	
Christianity	236.24
Heavenly bodies	520
folklore	398
Hebrews (Biblical book)	227.87
Helicopters	
transportation services	387
Hell	
Christianity	236.25
Herbs	581
garden crop	635
Heredity	575
psychology	155
Heredity versus environment	
psychology	155.2

Heresy	
Christianity	262
Hermeneutics	
sacred books	
Bible	220.6
Heroes	
folklore	398
Hibernation	591
High blood pressure	
medicine	616
High-carbohydrate	613.2
High-fiber diet	613.2
High schools	373
Higher education	378
Highway accidents	363.12
Highway transportation	388.3
Highways	388.1
engineering	625
Hiking	796.5
Hill climbing	796.5
Hinduism	294.5
Hippies	305.5
Historical books (Old Testament)	222
History	900
Biblical events	220.9
world	909
Hobbies	
recreation	790.1
Hockey (Field sports)	796.3
Hockey (Ice sports)	796.9
Holidays	394.2
Holiness	
Christian doctrine	234
Holocaust (European history)	940
Holy Communion	234
public worship	264
Holy days	
Christianity	263
customs	394.2
Holy Spirit	231
Holy Trinity	231.044
Holy Week	263
devotional literature	242.35
Home appliances	643
Home buying	643

I

Kitchen utensils	641.5
Kitchens	643
Kites	629.1
recreation	796.1
Knitting	
arts	746.43
Knowledge	
psychology	153.4
Koran	297

L

Labor	331
Laity (Church members)	262
Lake transportation	386
Lakes	551
Lamentations (Bible)	224.3
Land transportation	388
Land use	333
agricultural surveys	631.4
Landforms	551.4
Landscape architecture	712
Landscape design	712
Language	400
Language groups	
(Sociology)	305.7
Laser communications	
engineering	621
Lasers	621
Last Judgment	
Christianity	236
Latin America	980
Latin language	470
Latin literature	870
Latter-Day Saints Church	289.3
Law	340
Law enforcement	363.2
Lawns	
floriculture	635.9
landscape architecture	712
Leadership	303.3
psychology	158
Learning	
educational psychology	370
psychology	153.1
Learning disabilities	371.9
medicine	616.85

Leather	
handicrafts	745.5
Leaves (Plants)	
physiology	581.1
Left-and right-handedness	
psychology	152.3
Legal aid	362.5
Legal ethics	174
Legends	
folklore	398
Leisure	
recreational arts	790
Lent	263
Lettering	
decorative arts	745.6
Letters (Correspondence)	
etiquette	395
Leviticus	222.13
Liability insurance	368
Libraries	027
Library acquisitions	025.2
Library administration	025.1
Library catalogs	025.3
Library networks	021
Library science	020
Life	
origin	
religion	
Christianity	231.7
Life after death	
religion	
Christianity	236
Life insurance	368
Life sciences	570
Lifelong education	374
Light	535
art	701
engineering	621
Lighthouses	387
Lighting	621.32
architectural design	729
Lighting fixtures	
household management	645
Lightning	551.5
Limericks	808.8
Linguistics	410

Nonverbal communication	302.2
psychology	153.6
Nonviolence	303.6
North America	970
North Americans	970
civilization	970
social group	305.8
Nose	
human diseases	
medicine	616
human physiology	612.2
Nuclear energy	333.79
Numbers	510
Numbers (Biblical book)	222.14
Nurse and patient	610.7
Nurseries (For plants)	631.5
horticulture	635
Nursery rhymes	398.8
Nursery school	372
Nurses	610.7
role and function	610.7
Nursing	
home economics	649.8
medicine	610.7
Nursing (Breast feeding)	649
Nursing homes	362.1
Nutrition	363.8
health	613.2
home economics	641.1
Nuts	582
orchard crop	634

O

Obadiah (Biblical book)	224.91
Obedience	
Christian salvation	234.6
Obesity	
dietetics	613.2
Obscenity	
ethics	176
social problem	363
Obstetrics	618.2
Occultism	133
religious practice	291.3
Occupational education	370
Occupational ethics	174

Occupational guidance	331.7
Occupational therapy	615.8
Occupational training	
adult education	374
secondary education	373
Occupations	331.7
Ocean	551.46
Octopus	594
Oil (Petroleum)	553
Old age	305.26
Old persons	305.26
geriatrics	618.97
physiology	612.6
psychology	155.67
social welfare	362.6
Old Testament	221
Biography	221.92
Olympic Games	796
On-the-job training	331.2
Online catalogs	025.3
Online information systems	025
Only child	306.874
psychology	155.44
Opera	782
Ophthalmology	617
Optical illusions	
psychology	152.14
Optometry	617
Oral communication	302.2
Oral contraceptives	
health	613.9
Oral hygiene	617.6
Orchards	634
Orchestra	784.2
Organ (Musical instrument)	786.5
Organ transplants	
surgery	617
Organic farming	631.5
Organization (Management)	658
Orient	950
Oriental languages	490
Original sin	233.1
Orphans	
social services	362.7
Orthodontics	617.6
Osteoporosis	
medicine	616.7

Peanuts	641.3
garden crop	635
Peas	641.3
garden crop	635
Peasants	305.5
Pediatrics	618.92
Penance	
Christianity	234
Penmanship	652
Pensions	331.2
Pentateuch	222
Pentecostal churches	289.9
Perception	
psychology	153.7
sensory	152.1
Percussion instruments	786.8
Performances	790
music	780
Performing arts	790
Perfumes	
customs	391
Persecutions	
Christian church history	272
Personal appearance	646.7
customs	391
Personal computers	004.1
programming	005.1
Personal finance	332.024
home economics	640
Personal health	613
Personal hygiene	613
Personal improvement	646.7
applied psychology	158
Personal living	646.7
Personal names	929.4
Personal religion	
Christianity	240
Personal safety	613.6
Personality	155.2
applied psychology	158
children	155.4
Personality disorders	
medicine	616.85
Personality tests	155.2
Personnel management	658
Perspective	
art	701

Persuasion	303.3
Pest control	363
agriculture	632
household sanitation	648
Peter (Biblical books)	227.9
Petroleum	553
Pets	636.088
Pharmacology	615
Philanthropy	
ethics	177
Philemon (Biblical book)	227.86
Philippians (Biblical book)	227.6
Philosophy	100
Phobias	
medicine	616.85
Phonics (Reading instruction)	
applied linguistics	418
elementary education	372
Photographs	770
Photography	770
Phrase books	418
Physical education	796
health	613.7
Physical fitness	613.7
Physical illness	362.1
Physical therapy	615.8
Physically handicapped persons	
social welfare	362.4
Physician and patient	610
Physicians	
role and function	610
Physics	530
engineering	621
Piano	786.2
Picnics	642
Picture dictionaries	413
Pictures	
fine arts	760
Piloting	
aeronautics	629.1
Place names	910
Plague	
medicine	616
Plains	551.4
Planetariums	520

Presbyterian church	285
Preschool children	305.23
psychology	155.4
Preschool education	372
Preventive medicine	613
Priesthood of Jesus Christ	232
Primers (Readers)	418
Princes	
folklore	398
Princesses	
folklore	398
Print media	
social aspects	302.23
Privacy	323
Private colleges	378
Private schools	371
Private universities	378
Private welfare services	361.7
Problem solving	153.4
Product development	
management	658
Product safety	363.1
Professional ethics	174
Professional sports	796
Professional writing	808
Professionals	305.5
Professions	331.7
Profit	338
Programmed instruction	371.3
Programming (Computers)	005.1
Programs (Computer)	005.3
Progress	303.4
Pronunciation	
applied linguistics	418
Propaganda	303.3
Property	330
Prophecies	
religion	
Biblical	220.15
Prophetic books (Old	
Testament)	224
Prophets (Biblical	
books)	224
Protestantism	280
Proverbs (Biblical book)	223.7
Providence of God	
Christianity	231

Psalms	223.2
Psalters	264
Pseudepigrapha	229
Psychiatric social work	362.2
Psychiatry	616.89
Psychology	150
Psychology of education	370
Psychoses	362.2
medicine	616.89
social welfare	362.2
Psychosomatic medicine	616
Psychotherapy	
psychiatry	616.89
Puberty	612.6
Public buildings	
architecture	725
Public colleges	378
Public education	371
Public health	362.1
Public housing	363.5
Public libraries	027.4
Public opinion	303.3
Public relations	659
local churches	254.4
Public safety	363.1
Public schools	371
Public speaking	808.5
Public universities	378
Public worship	
Christianity	264
Judaism	296.4
Pumpkins	641.3
Punctuation	411
Puppets	791.5
Purgatory	
Christianity	236.5
Puritanism	285
Purses	391
Puzzles	793.73

Q

Quackery	
medicine	615.8
Quakers	289.6
Quality of life	
sociology	306

Religious freedom	323	Rest	
Christianity	261.72	physical fitness	613.7
Judaism	296.3	Rest homes	362.1
Religious life		Restoration	
Christianity	248.4	architecture	720
comparative religion	291.4	Resume' writing	808
Judaism	296.7	Resurrection	
Religious plays		Christianity	236.8
literature	808.82	Judaism	296.3
stage presentation	792	Resurrection of Jesus	
Religious symbolism		Christ	232.97
Christianity	246	Retarded persons	
Judaism	296.4	social welfare	362.3
painting	755	Retarded students	371.9
Remarriage	306.84	Retired persons	305.9
Remedial reading	418	psychology	155.67
elementary education	372	Retirement	306.3
Reminiscences	920	financial planning	332.024
Remodeling of buildings	690	psychology	155.67
architecture	720	Retirement guides	646.7
by homemaker	643	Retirement income	
Renaissance period		pensions	331.2
(European history)	940	Retreats (Religion)	
Renovation of buildings	690	Christianity	269.6
architecture	720	Revelation (Biblical book)	228
Rent	333	Revelation of God	
Renting homes	643	Christianity	231.7
Repairing	620	Judaism	296.3
home economics	643	Revival meetings	269
Repentance		Revolution	
Christianity	234.5	social change	303.4
Judaism	296.3	sociology	303.6
Representation		Revolutionary War	
political right	323	U.S. history	970
Reproduction	574.1	Rhetoric	808
animals	591	Rhyme	808
human physiology	612.6	Rhymes	
plants	581.1	folk literature	398.8
Reptiles	597.9	Rhyming games	398.8
Rescue operations	363	Rhythm (Music)	781.2
Residential buildings	643	Rich (Social class)	305.5
architecture	728	Riddles	398.6
home economics	643	Riding (Horsemanship)	798.2
Respiratory system	591	Right and wrong	170
animal physiology	591	Right of assembly	323
human diseases	616.2	Right to die	
human physiology	612.2	ethics	179

S

Satellites (Moons)	523.9	Secondary education	373
Satire	808.8	Secondary schools	373
Saturn (Planet)	523.4	Sects (Religion)	
Savings	332	Christianity	280
personal finance	332.024	Judaism	296.8
Schizophrenia		Secular voice music	782
medicine	616.89	Secularism	211.6
Scholarships	371.2	Securities	332.6
higher education	378	Seed-bearing plants	582
Scholastic Aptitude Test	378	Seedless plants	586
School and home	370	Seeds	582
School and society	370	agriculture	631.5
School buildings	371.6	Segregation in education	370
School calendar	371.2	Self	
School children	305.23	psychology	155.2
psychology	155.4	Self-actualization	155.2
School day	371.2	applied psychology	158
School discipline	371.5	Self-care (Health)	613
School dropouts	371.2	Self-confidence	155.2
School facilities	371.6	applied psychology	158
School libraries	027.8	Self-control	179
School lunch programs	371.7	psychology	153.8
School orchestra	784	Self-defense	613.6
School organization	371	Self-development	
School safety programs	371.7	adult education	374
School systems	371	applied psychology	158
Schooling	370	Self-esteem	155.2
Schools	371	applied psychology	158
Science	500	Self-instruction	371.3
Science and religion		Self-respect	155.2
Christianity	261.5	applied psychology	158
Judaism	296.3	Selfishness	179
Scissors	621	Selling	
Scores (Music)	780	commerce	380
Scouting	369	management	658
Scripture readings		Seminaries	
public worship		Christianity	207.1
Christianity	264	Seminars	371.3
Scuba diving		Senior citizens	305.26
sports	797.2	Senior high schools	373
Sculpture	730	Seniority	
Sea	551.46	labor economics	331.2
Seafood	641.3	Sensation	
Seaports	387	psychology	152.1
Seashore	551.4	Sense organs	591
Seashore ecology	574.5	animal physiology	591
Seasons	508	human physiology	612.8

psychology	155.9
String orchestra	784
Stringed instruments	787
Stroke (Disorder)	
medicine	616
Student activities	371.8
Student aid	371.2
Student discipline	371.5
Student exchanges	370
Student life	371.8
Student loans	371.2
Students	371.8
Student groups	
adult education	374
Stuffed toys	
making	680
handicrafts	745.5
Stuttering	
medicine	616.85
special education	371.9
Style	
art	701
Style manuals	808
Subject cataloging	025.4
Subject indexing	025.4
Substance abuse	362.29
Substitute teaching	371.1
Suburbs	307.74
Subways	388
Success	646.7
applied psychology	158
Success in business	650.1
Suffrage	324
Suicide	362.2
Summer	508
Summer school	371.2
Sun	523.7
Sunday	
Christian observance	263.4
Sunday school	268
Judaism	296.6
Sundials	680
Supernatural beings	
folklore	398
Superstitions	
folklore	398

Supervision	
personnel management	658
Supper	642
Surfing	797.3
Surgery	617
Surgical nursing	
medicine	610.7
Surrogate motherhood	
ethics	176
Survival skills	613.6
Swimming	797.2
physical fitness	613.7
Symbolism	
religious significance	
Christianity	246
Judaism	296.4
Symbols	302.2
Symphony orchestra	784.2
Symptoms	616
Synagogues	296.6
architecture	726
Synthesizer (Musical instrument)	786.7

T

Table linens	642
Table manners	395
Table service	642
Table tennis	796.3
Tailoring	646.4
Tapestries	
textile arts	746.3
Taste	591
human physiology	612.8
psychology	152.1
Tatting	
arts	746.43
Taxes	336.2
Taxicabs	388.3
Tea	641.3
Tea (Meal)	642
Teacher-parent relations	371.1
Teaching	371.1
Teaching aids	371.3
Teaching methods	371.3
Technical processing	
(Libraries)	025

Touch	
human physiology	612.8
psychology	152.1
Tourism	338
Towels	643
Towers (Structures)	
architecture	725
Towns	307.76
Toys	790.1
product safety	363.1
use in child care	649
Track (Sports)	796.4
Tractor trailers	
engineering	629.2
transportation services	388.3
Tractors	629.2
Traffic accidents	363.12
Traffic control	388
Traffic safety	363.12
Traffic signs	388.3
Train accidents	363.12
Training	
personnel management	658
Training of children	649
Trains	385
Tramps	305.5
Tramways	388
Translating	418
Translators	418
Transmission of	
electricity	621
Transportation	388
cause of social change	303.48
Transportation accidents	363.12
Transportation insurance	368
Transportation safety	363.12
Travel	910
Travel guides	910.2
Trees	582
forestry	634
Trial by jury	
civil right	323
Trick games	793
Trinity	231.044
Triplets	306.875
Trolleys	388
Trucks	388.3

Trumpet	788
Tuition	371.2
higher education	378
Tunnels	388
Turtles	597.92
Tutoring	371.3
Twins	306.875
psychology	155.44
Typewriting	652.3

U

Umbrellas	391
Unemployment	331.1
Unemployment compensation	331.2
Unemployment insurance	368
UNICEF (Children's Fund)	362.7
Unicorns	398
Unification Church	289.9
Uniforms	391
Unitarian churches	289.1
United Brethren in Christ	289.9
United States	973
Universalist churches	289.1
Universe	
astronomy	523.1
Universities	378
University administration	378
University buildings	
architecture	727
University libraries	027.7
Unmarried mothers	306.874
Upholstery	
interior decoration	747
Upper classes	305.5
Urban areas	307.76
Urban development	307.1
Urban-rural migration	307.2
Urban sociology	307.76
Urban transportation	388
Usage (Linguistics)	418

V

V.C.R. (Cassette recorders)	384.55
Vacation homes	643
Vaccines	615
Valleys	551.4

Z